THE MONEY HOUSE

Dave Beckwith

Copyright © Dave Beckwith 2021
All Rights Reserved

TABLE OF CONTENTS

Introduction 7
CHAPTER I: Build your Moneyhouse 10
    THE MONEYHOUSE 11
    TAKE THE JOURNEY 13
    WHERE TO START 16
    TRACK 17
    Profile #1 TO BUY OR NOT TO BUY 21
CHAPTER II: Change the dreaded "Budget" word to Blueprint 24
    WHY BOTHER? 26
    A VISUAL AID 27
    CREATING THE BUDGET 30
    ENVELOPES 36
    THE UNFORESEEN 37
    Profile #2 WHERE DID THE MONEY GO? 40
CHAPTER III: Learn the art of saving 43
    ACCOUNTS 43
    SAVE! 47
    WHERE TO START 50
    THE BEST WAY TO SAVE 52
    Profile #3 RE-ARRANGED PRIORITIES 55
CHAPTER IV: Break the Chains to attain Freedom .. 59
    DUMP THE DEBT 59

DREAM AND VISUALIZE 64

DROWNING IN DEBT 66

CREDIT CARDS 71

Profile #4 MISSED OPPORTUNITIES 75

CHAPTER V: How to Maintain Accounts 78

THE BALANCE SECTION 81

DEPOSITS AND CREDITS 82

CHECKS 82

MISCELLANEOUS DEBITS 83

HOW TO RECONCILE THE BANK'S NUMBERS
WITH YOUR NUMBERS 83

ELECTRONIC TRANSACTIONS 88

BALANCE TOO LOW? 89

BALANCE TOO HIGH? 91

CELEBRATE! 91

ADDITIONAL THOUGHTS 92

Profile #5 WHEN THE INCOME STOPS 94

CHAPTER VI: Big Ticket Items 99

HOUSES 100

HELOCS 102

STAY IN DEBT OR DEBT FREE? 103

PAY TWICE 104

BUY WHAT YOU CAN AFFORD 106

CARS 108

LEASES 109

INVESTMENTS AND RETIREMENT 110

COLLEGE	112
STUDENT LOANS	114
WORK	115
FREE MONEY	116
IVY LEAGUE OR STATE?	116
Profile #6 THE COST OF PEER PRESSURE	118
Chapter VII: Keeping it Going!	124
FRUGALITY	127
BUYING USED	129
OPTIONS	130
MINIMALISM	133
GIVE IT AWAY	135
Profile #7 WHERE'S ALL THE MONEY?	137
Acknowledgments	140

Introduction

A skyscraper in San Francisco has many worried. The fifty eight story structure has sunk sixteen inches since completion in 2005. Settling is normal but this is excessive.

Even worse, it's beginning to lean. The Millennium Tower moved six inches toward a neighboring building. Finger pointing and blame shifting began in earnest as experts search for a solution. Fault lines in the area make the situation more problematic.

Pondering the skyscraper, it occurred to me it's similar to people's personal finances. Many are unsure how to fix an inherent defect. Residents in the tower are as troubled as the ones living through a bankruptcy or foreclosure.

Both problems have a common issue: the foundation.

Many Americans have an insufficient, sandy basis of financial knowledge on which to build their lives. They partially understand concepts, but forge ahead because it's how their friends do it. Following the lead of co-workers or relatives can be risky.

Our society is rich in information, but poor at walking alongside explaining details. Sometimes, basic skills fail to be taught because well, they're basic. They seem so commonplace and unnecessary to discuss.

In school we learned languages we seldom speak, about places we may never visit and elements of the periodic table that never serve us in our practical lives. We didn't learn how to balance a checkbook, make a budget work or how to save money for the future. Real life knowledge navigates us through the world.

We missed the informational session about money, or we lost the handout explaining it all. Maybe we were in the back row, talking to friends and not listening to the instructions.

After we're out in the world, it's difficult to rewind and find necessary information. Now we're too embarrassed to ask. Hence, the purpose of this small book. It fills the gap of what Mom and Dad forgot to teach about money management.

It is *not* an exhaustive treatise on money or investments. While I am a financial coach, this isn't repackaged theory from a textbook. I have walked every step of it and learned much by trial and error.

A warning: It is unconvoluted and rather simple, but it works. Some folks seek a new and exhilarating formula. This guide is neither. It is straightforward, clean and quiet. It is how your grandparents probably managed their finances. It isn't sexy or cutting edge, maybe even boring. But it works.

I dislike money stress so it's eliminated from my life. My marriage and home are peaceful now, but they weren't always.

Money touches every aspect of our lives. Managing it well will increase the quality of our relationships, determine the size of our dreams and add tranquility to our days. It's worth every effort to manage it well. My hope is to shed light on a dark, foreboding path, bring confidence in finances, and be a springboard to bigger and better things. Success prepares for and inspires other successes.

At the end of each chapter, I have profiled real individuals and tell you their money story. Some show in detail what not to do, while others showcase the courage and fortitude of stepping out of the mainstream and doing things their way. My hope is this book will be of great benefit and value to you.

CHAPTER I
Build your Moneyhouse

If we command our wealth, we shall be rich and free; if our wealth commands us, we are poor indeed.

— *Edmund Burke*

Have you ever imagined winning the lottery and being granted a new outlook on the world? What would you do if suddenly you were able to do anything you desired? Buy a home or take a long vacation?

The thought occurs to us at one time or another. It's fun to talk about but leaves us disappointed. Reality makes us sigh, as we realize 'That will never happen.'

As the old adage goes: I have good news and bad news.

The bad news is that you are correct. That *will* never happen. If people understood the astronomical odds of winning the lottery, most wouldn't risk their five dollar bill. They could just as well feed it into the paper shredder at the office for shock value; or maybe crack the window on the freeway and let it fly just to see it flutter in traffic. The financial benefit is identical.

So what's the good news? Your dreams and goals aren't decided by a one in a million random chance. What a miserable, dismal outlook you would face if that were true. No, they are attainable. You can't decide who wins the Power Ball, but the joystick of your destiny is in your hands.

Since planets won't align to bring you instant wealth, it's important to know you can create a desirable life one block at a time. It's hard work but possible. I suggest dreaming of what you would love to do or have, and logically take steps toward it. If you only achieve three quarters of the goal, you still are farther ahead than most people and even yourself had you never made the attempt.

THE MONEYHOUSE

Think of the financial situation you'd like to have as a house you build. There are many parallels between the two. A home provides somewhere to be at the end of the day, a comfortable space to be yourself in. It keeps you off the street. Your castle protects you from the elements. You can be warm, dry and comfortable while a blinding snowstorm rages outside.

A fine home usually appreciates in value; it's where life's memories are made.

Handling money well offers similar benefits. When dollars go where they are needed, it brings an element of peace and rest to our lives. The nagging sense of a task left undone is removed. Life brings enough stress from things we can't control, the area of money shouldn't be one of them.

Just like a brick and mortar residence, good financial skills will keep you protected from cloudbursts that surprise us, and provide a haven against a bad economy. Regular saving is a port in the storm many wish they had. Good habits bring peace and security when things get crazy in our world.

Also like the homestead you leave your grandchildren someday, sound money management blesses people around you in a profound way, as well as those to come many years from now. This competence is worth learning well.

You may say 'Well, that sounds great. What good is a 'pie in the sky'? How can I actually get there?'

TAKE THE JOURNEY

That's the purpose of this book. A long journey begins with a single step. You can arrive anywhere you want to be if you know the way and take the steps. Many successful people began with very little or nothing. Being broke is no barrier to a life you're proud of if you commit to getting there. But most people won't make the commitment. The average American survives from one payday to the next. They have little saved with mounting debts. In the wealthiest nation on the planet, this is unnecessary and avoidable. The first takeaway here is: don't follow the crowd. They have no idea how to do this well. A 'path less traveled' can lead to wealth and contentment.

Imagine living the life you desire. Have a vision for the future. Be determined to achieve it.

If you decide to build a real house, you will encounter obstacles. There may be blueprints for which you need clarification, mistakes that need corrected, items requiring more money than anticipated and difficulties you couldn't foresee.

Why would anyone take on such a project? It's insanity.

Because it's worth it. Many years from now, while enjoying a cold drink on the rear deck as the sun sets, you will barely recall the sacrifices it took to place you in a great spot less determined people will never reach.

It's not an easy 'walk in broke, walk out rich' scenario. A life worth having requires more work and forethought. There's more good news. Many people who have already blazed the trail are willing to share their secrets. Information is available. The wise seek the know-how, and adapt it to their situations.

You may need to start small, and upgrade over time, as you would with a real structure. It takes time and patience. One doesn't toss up a fine two story brick home on a long weekend. Neither will you be on a perfect budget, tweaked to the penny and out of debt the first month.

This guide will provide tools and information,

dispel incorrect notions, and replace your nagging sense of unrest with contentment. Peace of mind is a beautiful thing. It's not just for a select few, but all of us. P. T. Barnum said that "Money is a terrible master, but an excellent servant." So true.

Pressures mount when funds won't cover expenses. It causes stress, frustration, short tempers and harsh words. However, with proper management, these tend to go away.

We are fortunate to live in the information age. Money help abounds. But with so many contributors, it's not always good advice. Author and business giant Brian Buffini says that we are awash in information but starving for wisdom.

It's true. Our world is great at providing information, but terrible at walking beside and explaining the details.

Consequently, many struggle with what appears to be a simple skill. Self esteem suffers when intelligent people have difficulty paying bills on time and saving money.

I know I had a rough time. I grew up observing my Mom handle the household finances. She was a single mom in the seventies before it was commonplace. No aid was available so she couldn't afford mistakes. She separated cash into envelopes, paid the bills due that week, and busied herself with other matters, like keeping me in line. It looked easy.

When I moved out and got married, I wanted to imitate Mom's efficiency. Unfortunately, casual observers miss important details; I fell flat on my face.

For years there never seemed to be enough money, I was constantly working, and constantly short of cash. My marriage suffered through many money fights, assuming my wife was blowing money when I was trying so hard, while she thought I was the problem. We were both wrong.

I learned that finger pointing and blame shifting took more energy than devising a plan.

It's a comfort to know you can go from clueless to competent with the right help.

WHERE TO START

The first place to begin is in your mind. Henry Ford said "If you think you can do a thing or think you can't do a thing, you're right". This is absolutely true and a great place to launch your journey to financial proficiency. Know you have the intelligence and drive to do this well. The wisest man on earth, King

Solomon said it this way: "As a man thinks in his heart, so he is." That's basically the same thing Mr. Ford said, just a few thousand years earlier. Who am I to argue with men of such caliber?

The point is this is very do-able. You don't need to re-invent the wheel. It's good to keep it simple. Many in our world want to complicate money management, invent terms to inflate the ego and cause us to feel like we're in the smarty group, (the dummies are over there avoiding debt and piling up cash) and we toss terms around we only somewhat understand. Be impressed with a rising account balance instead of the headiness of IPO, stock options or hedge funds.

As wealth increases, become as fluent as you can. But today, learn to walk well before signing up for the marathon. Be adept at managing what you have now.

TRACK

A great place to start is by tracking expenses. This provides information to make your plan, shows exactly how each dollar is spent. Your list of expenditures is your reference point to create the best spending plan for your personal economy.

It's like going to a new mall and finding the directory which shows a red dot saying "You Are Here." The Food Court is to the left, the restrooms are straight ahead, and your favorite store is on the upper level. Now you can decide where to go next.

Tracking expenses does the same thing. I found I tended to estimate, guess, or not consider some expenses. Without a receipt, I often forgot what I spent. So keeping the amounts recorded matters. Numbers need to be accurate to build a straight, square house.

Everything you spend in a month should be written down. Sound like a pain in the neck?

It is. But hopefully, only one month is necessary. If you do it well, you'll find it's a reasonable sacrifice to get your finances in order to not fret over bills. Use a spiral notepad or your smartphone. There are apps that could simplify the process, use whatever works for you. But don't skip anything, no matter how small.

After one month, take your information and separate the amounts into categories: groceries, transportation, rent or mortgage, entertainment, etc. Create as many categories as necessary. Total each one, then give it an honest evaluation.

Most people find at least one area where they

spend more money than they realized. Have you ever wondered 'Where does all the money go?' This one month exercise will help you find the answer.

As a caffeine addict content to remain in addiction, seeing how much I spent on coffee was a little unsettling. Every work day I spent two or three dollars for coffee, a tiny fraction of my daily income. It was hard to imagine a small amount would make much difference. It doesn't for just one day, but when I considered the monthly amount and figured the yearly total—ouch. A lot more than I thought.

Tracking expenses is the predecessor to the actual budget. It's like drawing the blueprints and laying the foundation of the money house you want to build. So, when reviewing, consider what would be the least painful to cut or would benefit the most. Brewing coffee at home instead of stopping at a trendy coffee shop could save a bundle of cash. Brownbagging last night's leftovers will save you from buying lunch out. Or you might choose a more significant change like eliminating a car payment by purchasing an older car outright. Ways to trim expenses are there if you look.

Take the time necessary to record your transactions carefully and with notes and details.

Near the end of the month, it may be hard to remember what you purchased weeks ago.

Proper perspective is important here. The purpose is to formulate a working budget. Tracking looks behind you to figure out how much was spent but a budget looks forward to the next month. An accurate plan for the near future is the ultimate goal that tracking expenses will help you arrive at, but for clarity, knowing where it went isn't the same as a budget for moving forward, only a guideline.

Be excited about taking this first step. Keep in mind it's a journey. Be patient and expect setbacks to avoid discouragement when they appear. And remember, you can do this.

- Believe. Know it's possible to achieve above average things.
- Create a plan. List priorities and decide to develop a plan.
- Take the first step. Track expenses to lay the groundwork for a workable budget.

Profile #1
TO BUY OR NOT TO BUY

After his divorce in 2006, Bill moved to Georgia and landed a job, excited about his fresh start. High home prices frustrated his goal of home ownership. Conservative with money, he was reluctant to get in over his head with a large monthly payment.

His tax preparer suggested using money from his 401k retirement savings as a larger down payment to lower his mortgage loan. It seemed better than borrowing.

As he considered his options, housing prices were leveling off after years of rising. Some speculated they might fall. Others assumed it was only a lull and costs would continue to rise. There were good arguments from both perspectives.

Since every decision contains an element of uncertainty, Bill took the tax preparer's advice, withdrew from savings, and bought the house he found.

In the following years, the housing market crashed and took a decade to recover.

I don't want to beat up our friend. No one can predict the future. Bill was caught in unfortunate timing with many others.

But, he made a few fatal and avoidable errors. First, he took advice for the wrong reasons. His tax preparer *was* a great guy. They had good rapport and had done business together for years. His friend was a professional. Bill never had a problem with a tax return. However, the man's expertise was *taxes,* not real estate or finances. In those areas, he simply had ideas.

Bill granted him the same confidence in a field in which he merely held an opinion.

I may write well, but you'd be quite unhappy if you hired me to fix the brakes on your car. You'd be contacting a lawyer or getting a bulk discount on trunks and bumpers..

It's wise to get several opinions when considering large purchases you'll pay on for many years. Use caution when spending carefully saved money.

While the additional down payment lowered Bill's monthly installment, an ugly consequence remained. A 401k is structured to grow tax free until retirement. Withdrawing money before retirement age adds fees and penalties. In addition, the funds count as taxable income.

Worst of all, growth the money would have gained in the marketplace for years to come is GONE. A horrible deal. It's like getting a loan with a 28-30% interest rate—a choice few would make.

Bill's blunder had its roots in something we're all guilty of at one time or another. Impatience. House fever made him antsy, and he bought while the prices were fluctuating. They eventually came *way* down. Had he exercised self-restraint, waited and watched the market patterns a little longer, he wouldn't have needed the retirement savings. He could have owned the same house for a low payment without the loss or penalties.

Learning from others' mistakes can save money and pain.

CHAPTER II
Change the dreaded "Budget" word to Blueprint

The person who doesn't know where his next dollar is coming from usually doesn't know where his last dollar went.
— Unknown

As you track expenses you'll gain a sense of where resources flow to, and be able to tell which category needs restricted and what needs increased. The next step is to create a budget. We want to add tools to your toolbox that you'll need to build the financial house of your dreams.

Many tense up at the word "budget." It feels claustrophobic and sounds intimidating. Call it your personal "spending plan" if it suits you better. That's all a budget is. You're deciding *before* you have the money, where it will go. It's much different than figuring how to cover all the expenses with what's left after a weekend of spending. I know how that works— not very well, since I've done it.

No two spending plans are alike. A college student with a grant or scholarship must plan for his money to last until the end of the semester or school year. He may supplement with a part time job or money from parents.

Someone with a full time job and a weekly paycheck will have a much different plan.

Customize your budget to your income stream and situation. All of them have basic elements in common to answer questions like;

1. How much money do you have to work with?
2. How long does it need to last before it is replenished?
3. What needs to be purchased with that finite amount?
4. In the event the money is spent before everything is purchased, what takes priority over less important items on the list?

This is why tracking expenses proves helpful. Before you can answer any of those questions, you need to know where you spend your money now.

WHY BOTHER?

So why would you restrict yourself to a budget? Perhaps you're a non-conformist or a maverick who takes life as it comes and doesn't like to plan weeks in advance. It may feel like intentionally subjecting yourself to a tyrant. What rational person would do that?

I understand. Let me offer a little perspective.

Approach your plan from different angle. First, it shields you from surprises. Not the kind your friends give you on your birthday. It protects against the bad kind, like the bank letter informing of a problem with your account. Errors in your favor only happen in Monopoly. A budget keeps a tight rein on money, reducing the chance of an NSF (Not Sufficient Funds) notice along with charges and fees.

Second, budgets reduce stress. When dollars are directed to planned expenses, services aren't paid late or turned off, and if you have some fun on the weekend, there's no angst because it's intentional. There's less to argue about if you share your home and budget. Leave stress to things you have no control over.

Third, budgets build confidence when your spending plan works. Now *you're* the one who has things together and it feels great. Many people pretend to be smart and successful, but their finances are chaotic. As a money coach, I've met people whose lives look amazing but are in shambles behind the scenes. Learning to budget allows you to *truly* have things running like a well oiled machine.

Fourth, if you have children now, or expect to someday, a peaceful home is a great gift to them. Not to mention money aptitude is a wonderful skill to leave as a legacy.

Fifth, the extreme benefit is to avoid the embarrassment and expense of having terminated services turned back on. It's awkward to ask a friend if you can use their shower. A good spending plan can be compared to a fence in your yard protecting a child. You aren't treating him like an animal, you're preventing him from walking into dangerous traffic. A budget is a boundary for your money. There are more reasons to budget, but you get the point.

A VISUAL AID

What's next? Create a blank calendar month and pencil in the expenses on the date they're due. It allows you to see at a glance which bill is due and when, and how much it costs.

The rent or mortgage may be due on the first. Perhaps the cell phone bill is due week two. Insert your utilities and loan payments in the appropriate places. Ascertain which commitments must be met from each paycheck. If you're paid once a month, everything must be met from one check. Customize your bill paying to your income stream.

In addition to the recurring monthly payments, you need money for daily needs like food and gas for your car. Everything must be incorporated to make this work in real life. If you balance to the penny but forget groceries, it simply won't work. Eating trumps the cable bill.

A "generic" calendar month is great for visual learners. With one glance, you immediately know what to allocate money for in the time period. It's easy to see when money will be needed for a particular obligation.

Remember expenses not paid monthly. For example, car insurance may be due every three, six, or twelve months. Split up the amount monthly so you can prepare for it. If it's $1200.00 per year, allocate $100.00 per month. When you allocate, you simply set it aside until the specific need arises or comes due.

The visual month is a great reference or reminder to pay each bill on time. It reduces anxiety, as well as avoiding unnecessary late charges.

Sunday	Monday	Tuesday	Wednesday	Thursday	Friday	Saturday

CREATING THE BUDGET

You now have two important tools. First, you have a record of your spending from last month, and a generic calendar month with bills written in on the due date.

It's time to build the actual budget. Since there are many different scenarios, we'll assume you are operating a small household and your job pays you every two weeks. Your net pay is $1500 for two weeks. It may look something like this:

RENT – $600.00

GROCERIES – $100.00

Week 1

GROCERIES – $100.00

Week 2

GASOLINE – $40.00

Week 1

GASOLINE – $40.00

Week 2

ELECTRIC BILL – $95.00

CELL PHONE – $72.00

ENTERTAINMENT/RESTAURANTS – $65.00

CHURCH/CHARITY – $120.00

MISCELLANEOUS – $25.00

HAIRCUT – $15.00

SAVINGS – $85.00

CREDIT CARD – $40.00

VETERINARIAN – $20.00

CAR INSURANCE – $20.00

CLOTHES – $40.00

GIFTS/BIRTHDAYS – $20.00

TOTAL – $1497.00 $3.00 SURPLUS

This is a simple example of a budget for a two week period. The next budget would show money being paid to other expenses due in the second half of the month, cable bill, trash etc. You could prepare a budget for the entire month or for each pay period, whichever works best for you.

Customize your plan to mirror your situation. Create as many categories as needed. You may have categories or expenses that won't get funded on every budget. For example, Veterinarian and Birthdays may receive money only when there's extra available or an approaching vet visit.

Notice that gasoline and groceries have an allocation for week one and week two. This is an additional boundary to stay to a fixed amount. You could combine them and have a single $200.00 groceries category. However, if you overspend on week one, you may have a three day fast at the end of week two. Wisdom would suggest splitting them to avoid it.

The same idea applies to rent or mortgage. Any opportunity to spread out an expense should be taken.

Here's one way to refashion your spending plan. We'll use George as an example. He's young, with few bills, and paid weekly.

His spending plan may look like this:

WEEK ONE-
Rent- $650.00
Cell phone- $60.00
Groceries- $60.00
Fuel and incidentals - $48.00 Total: $818.00
WEEK TWO-
Utilities (Water) - $45.00
Groceries- $60.00
Fuel and incidentals- $48.00 Total: $153.00
WEEK THREE-
Power Bill - $95.00
Groceries - $60.00
Fuel and incidentals - $48.00 Total: $203.00
WEEK FOUR-
Cable bill- $52.00

Groceries -$60.00

Car insurance- $54.00

Fuel and incidentals - $48.00 Total: $214.00

George earns $425 per week. This means he's hundreds of dollars in the hole in week one, flush with cash in week two and okay in weeks three and four. A good plan would eliminate the peaks and valleys and bring consistency. Happiness shouldn't rise and fall with your cash flow.

How can he level out his income and expenses? By looking ahead and devising a plan. Put away the surplus in the easy weeks, and add it to the lean weeks. If he divides his rent over the whole month, it would be $162.50 per week. It will take from the surplus in weeks two and three, but more importantly, it eliminates the shortage in week one. Take a look:

WEEK 1-

Rent - $162.50

Cell Phone - $60.00

Groceries- $60.00

Fuel and Incidentals- $48.00 Total- $330.50

Surplus: $94.50

WEEK 2-

Rent - $162.50

Utilities (Water) $45.00

Groceries - $60.00

Fuel and Incidentals - $48.00 Total- $315.50

Surplus: $109.50

WEEK 3-

Rent - $162.50

Power bill - $95.00

Groceries - $60.00

Fuel and Incidentals - $48.00 Total - $365.50

Surplus: $59.50

WEEK 4 -

Rent- $162.50

Cable bill -$52.00

Groceries - $60.00

Car Insurance - $54.00

Fuel and Incidentals - $48.00 Total - $376.50

Surplus: $ 48.50

Without earning a single dollar more, George will have a cash surplus each week simply by preparing for what's coming. Because most people pay the rent or mortgage monthly, the plan requires a phase in period to fully implement. This simplistic example applies to bigger numbers and more convoluted situations.

As you go deeper into the budget process, keep

this in mind. It will take two to three months to get it right. Even after you get it polished and near perfect, the unexpected will come from nowhere and throw your numbers off. Expect it and don't be discouraged. Persistence is key. A budget that didn't work like you hoped this month is still better than winging it without a plan.

A plan will help to trim spending in one area to be able to funnel more into a category that runs low. For example, if you find you overspend on restaurants, while the savings account hasn't grown in six months, set a limit on eating out to be able to save more.

Do everything in small incremental steps. Huge changes in spending may not work and leads to discouragement. Keep the drive and desire alive.

Scale back the restaurant category to a level you can handle. Try to stay within the boundaries you set. If you exceed the amount consistently, readjust the limit or try harder to make it work.

See the spending plan as a blueprint to answer all financial needs. A well balanced life will include fun and entertainment, saving for the future, a quality life in the present, and necessary items dealt with. A working budget will spread resources to all these areas. Each area may need more, but a limit is required to have all the needs being met to some degree.

Much of this is trial and error, experimenting to find what works best.

Lifestyle changes can be big savers to get the numbers to work. Bad habits aren't cheap. Mentioned earlier, the lottery can be a real drain on the budget. Forget the false hope and send money where it benefits more.

I spent years funding the tobacco companies as a smoker. A pack of my brand costs five to six dollars per pack. That's over $2500 in one year if you smoke a pack a day. Besides bringing cash to your plan, kicking the habit will reduce the chances of oxygen tanks in your future, not a bad trade. You'll find ways to save when you search for them.

ENVELOPES

What should you do with money that is earmarked for a need that doesn't arise very often, like birthdays?

There's a perfect solution that works every time. But, it's somewhat of a dinosaur. Cold hard cash. Keep money in envelopes, actual bills allocated for a specific purpose. A mini file box works well too. You can easily add or eliminate categories as needed.

In our electronic age, debit cards, credit cards and electronic funds transfers are common. But cash is a great tool to have and use. It's especially efficient for a budget and staying within a financial boundary. If there is an envelope marked "Date night" with $75.00 inside, you won't accidentally spend $30.00 of the rent money. The night is over when the $75.00 is gone.

With cash separated in a file for each category, you can have as many as needed and contribute any denomination. Birthdays mentioned above work great in the cash system.

THE UNFORESEEN

Once I was attempting to fill my gas tank when a storm knocked out the satellite link. Debit and credit cards didn't work. I always keep a twenty folded and tucked away in my wallet. Cash saved me from being stranded that day. Cash pays on demand and doesn't depend on technology to work.

My family lives on the Gulf coast of Florida. Hurricanes or tropical storms can threaten without much warning. Common sense and safety demand forethought. I have cash in a safe place at home in case we have to make a dash and escape a storm. It's enough to go inland and cover and a few nights in a motel. We haven't used it yet and may never, but it's there if an emergency crops up. I always encourage my coaching clients to incorporate cash into their plan somewhere.

Security is a benefit of intentional money management and forethought. You are prepared to handle what life throws at you. Anticipation of problems is a great habit to have. Expect the unexpected. Emergencies don't make appointments.

Another benefit of cash on hand is when you come across a rummage sale or roadside stand. You can find some bargains but the hologrammed debit card is of no value there.

Consider integrating cash into your money house. It doesn't make sense for everything though. The money for the power bill needs to be in your account to pay the bill, not in an envelope. Likewise with retirement saving. It needs to be in the marketplace, gaining interest and growing, not piling up in a desk drawer.

- Create a visual, generic calendar to anticipate bills due.
- Use the expense tracker to fashion a budget
- Incorporate cash into your plan.

Profile #2
WHERE DID THE MONEY GO?

Hank is middle aged and has worked at the same manufacturing plant since high school. His story is typical. Everyday he stops at a convenience store to pick up lunch, his morning coffee and a can of chewing tobacco. When he feels lucky, he'll buy a scratch off lottery ticket. Eighteen dollars poorer, he heads to work.

On Fridays, he and the guys stop for a drink before going home. Shop talk and stories gin up an appetite, so he'll order hot wings and treat the boys to another round. They deserve it after a long week.

Hank and his wife live in a mobile home they own, parked on a rented lot. They manage paycheck to paycheck, but have little money saved. Vacations require a small loan. Years of this lifestyle convinced them that "this is just the way it is for a working man."

Here's the point. Money mistakes aren't always a car or home that's too expensive. Far more often, daily habits subtly drain away resources. Operating without intentionality and a specific plan, money *will* mysteriously evaporate. Then we wonder what happened, why we're broke.

What did Hank do wrong? Nothing really major, not a gambling or cocaine addiction. None of the things we associate with people who work hard but have little to show for it. What he failed to do was take charge and make his money perform for him.

Consider parents who fail to correct their children. When the kids scream, and disrupt everyone in the room, the parents sometimes say nothing, hoping they'll tire soon. Meanwhile, everyone is uncomfortable.

Dollars are like children. Without boundaries on where your money can or cannot go, it will *not* behave, but will drift away. Restricting the amount you spend for each category prevents impulse buying that wastes resources.

This is important because we look at people who don't have much money with a distorted lens. Maybe they're lazy and should work a little more. Or perhaps they aren't too smart, we simply write them off as losers.

Let's look at Hank again. He's kept his plant position for decades because he performs well and works overtime. He's not lazy or stupid, but one of the best machine operators in his department. Happily married to the same lovely woman for decades, bosses and many friends think well of him. No one would call him a loser.

We all make blunders and have some lack of discipline. But never settle for mediocrity because you lack a five star income. Dollars saved from an entry level position are as valuable as those earned from a medical practice.

Money skills, like all skills are learned. Zig Ziglar said "Anything that is worth doing, is worth doing poorly until you get better at it." A failed attempt is better than one never tried.

CHAPTER III
Learn the art of saving

If you would be wealthy, think of saving as well as getting.

— *Benjamin Franklin*

ACCOUNTS

Your local bank or credit union offers several kinds of accounts. Each one has the fundamental function of storing money. The difference is the purpose for it.

For example, there's the basic checking account, which holds the funds to pay for daily needs of life. There is more activity in this account than the others, therefore, more possibility of a problem because of numerous transactions.

There are savings accounts to store money in the event you need more for unexpected expenses or something on your wish list.

Also available are money market accounts and Certificates of Deposit (CD). These accounts will tie up your funds or limit access to them for a pre-determined amount of time in return for a higher interest rate. These are the most common accounts a financial institution will offer.

There are also variations of each to suit your situation. The terms and conditions may vary slightly among different banks but the basics are similar. Don't be afraid to ask questions regarding fees or details that will affect your costs.

For example, some banks have limits on the number of checks that can be written per month. Some accounts require a minimum balance to be maintained. Charges apply if the balance falls below that amount.

Some accounts bear interest, others do not. Marble walls and that funny bank smell can make anyone feel small and broke. But *you* are the customer. They are there to serve you, so never be intimidated. Ask questions and know what to expect.

CNBC says that 25% of American households are

unbanked or underbanked, according to a 2017 survey. These are people who have no bank account or underutilize the ones they have. The reasons vary. The "unbanked" assume they don't have enough money to have an account. Some distrust banks or think it's cheaper to use money orders or prepaid debit cards to meet obligations. Many have been bitten by the overdraft fees charged by banks. For most, it's a lack of understanding, which makes the banking system seem overwhelming and scary.

A whole industry has been built for people without regular accounts. Payday loans, check cashing services, "buy here, pay here" car lots and bill paying services all exist to collect fees and outrageous interest rates from those who can least afford it.

Consumers pay more for these alternative methods. Check cashing services appear inexpensive compared to a $35 overdraft charge. The occasional money order fee *looks* reasonable alongside a "below the minimum balance" charge.

In reality, over the course of the year, it is significantly more. With the right information, anyone can be free of these sharks and competently handle a conventional account.

Many banks offer low cost or free accounts but downplay them simply because they're not profitable. If you are among the unbanked, please reconsider. An active account with a good financial institution is a huge money managing asset. It allows you to meet obligations simply and on time. With online access, you can easily monitor all transactions. As a financial coach, I walk folks through step by step to competently manage any account. The Rocky Mountains can be frightening territory, but a good outfitter can remove the trepidation. There is no shame in being unfamiliar with the geography and the associated risks. Coaches exist to help navigate the unknown.

If you really dislike banks, credit unions are a great option, they are smaller and more personal than a huge bank corporation. They are often locally based, with several account options. Because they are non-profit, the fees are generally lower than a standard bank.

But if you decide to have an account with a large national chain, dealing personally with the local branch regularly can bring great rewards. It's easier to conduct business with a familiar, friendly face. Build rapport with the tellers. I know of a bank employee personally calling an account holder to warn of an overdraft charge. They were able to cover the shortfall and avoid the charge. It's better when bankers associate a real face to a name. Most bankers are great people that want to help you keep your account up and running. Inquire and clarify anything confusing.

SAVE!

To attain real security, you must become a saver. Movie fans will recall the old westerns where a rancher would tie a mule to a post, and the animal would walk in circles all day to pump water from the well.

Sadly, many are on the same path with their finances. They work hard, try to be wise with resources, but still feel they are going around in circles, gaining nothing. This hopeless treadmill begins with a financial shortfall. They run out and in desperation borrow or use a credit card.

The following weeks see a shortfall from repaying the loan or card. Without a personal pool of money to draw from, the debtor will remain locked into the "run out, borrow, repay and run out" merry-go-round forever. This is unnecessary.

Many of us suffer from a distorted view of the world. While it may be noble to seek ideals, they are often the exception, not the rule.

Relating to finances, we plan for everything to go well for a long time. We may purchase a home out of our price range; raises are expected, debts get paid and we hope to grow into the payment.

What if a pink slip comes instead of a raise? What if a little one comes along and an income is reduced or eliminated?

Wisdom expects the unexpected. The motor in your car will break down someday. A storm could blow shingles off your roof. One misstep could suddenly leave you unable to work or walk for weeks.

This is not negative thinking; it's being prepared for the curve ball life throws at us. Having money saved takes the sting out of the punch to the nose.

It's smart to save for the unexpected, but also the expected ones as well. Your spouse's birthday will be here in less than a year. If you live in a cold place, you'll need fuel to keep warm this winter.

Christmas is more enjoyable when the shopping money has been saved all year, with no dread of starting the New Year broke and playing "catch up" until March.

If not preoccupied with lack of money, a sense of child-like wonder returns with the holiday lights and music.

This may seem foreign. As Americans we are generally poor at saving money. We are the wealthiest nation but bad at storing for later.

It hasn't always been this way.

The generation that fought World War II grew up during the Great Depression, giving them a firm grasp on living within their means. They witnessed firsthand how life could turn on a dime. Huge fortunes were lost in a single day.

Those hardships taught them to buy only when they had the money. If they had to borrow to purchase, they would do without until they could pay cash. Although we live in a different era, we ignore those lessons at our peril.

The unpredictable nature of life demands financial backup. Ready or not, those curveballs are coming. Far better to prepare before the crisis. One may say they can't afford to prepare, yet will somehow afford the emergency that arises. It's either "pay now or pay later". Nothing is gained by waiting until the emergency.

Preparation means you're ready for the battle—poised on the wall, weapon in hand in full armor; better than catching one in the back as you scramble, figuring what to do.

WHERE TO START

Imagine if tomorrow you were slammed with an increase in your power bill, or an unexpected surcharge or tax. After complaining or writing a letter, you would dig down and pay it.

Do the same here, but pay yourself. Pretend an expense is required and you have no option. The difference is instead of money disappearing down a rabbit hole, you actually benefit from this self-imposed charge. You may object and ask what will a lousy few dollars do for me? Excellent question! Let's explore that.

Of course, all situations are different, what's a large sum to one, another leaves as a tip. The amount saved isn't as important as the habit that will benefit your life in the years ahead.

Don't look so much at the dollar amount as the big picture. Successful people set goals and work towards them. There are setbacks, but it doesn't matter. Progress is made toward the ultimate goal.

Imagine you can realistically save ten dollars a week. That doesn't sound like much— only two lattes at the famous coffee place, or only two items a day from the value menu of a fast food joint. What will that accomplish?

Today, nothing. Climb high and gain a long-term perspective. You'll discover a year from now, you've accumulated $520 you only wish you had now. There's no interest to pay because it's yours.

Perhaps you can manage $50 per week. Even better. Next year will find you with $2600 at your disposal. There's another dynamic at work.

Once convinced of the need to save and how possible it is, you'll discover new ways to accomplish it. It's great to decide to change and see it happen. Results build excitement.

With confidence and a vision to save, you'll notice holes and cracks. Money holes that is; money cracks that leech away a little at a time, reducing the level of the cash tank. Most of it's still there so we don't worry much, life won't change over a tiny amount. But small expenditures add up over time. Each decision matters.

THE BEST WAY TO SAVE

The last point I'll make about saving is probably the best one. I've saved literally thousands of dollars over the years with this method. It's quite simple, nothing profound or complicated, the automatic deposit. Most of us are on the 'Direct Deposit' plan. Our employer deposits the paycheck electronically in the account we designate.

At my credit union, I prearranged it so when an electronic deposit occurs, immediately an amount I specify (and can change when I desire) is deposited in the account I choose.

For example: on payday, the institution automatically deposits part of the funds into savings, another amount to the Christmas club account. Sometimes a vacation club is offered I can opt for too.

It stings initially, but after a few months, you're accustomed to your new amount and the savings will grow.

When it's time to shop for Christmas or a problem arises, the issue is covered. It may be inconvenient, but not a major crisis since you've planned ahead. This intentional forethought saved me countless times.

The beauty of this is if you lack discipline, dollars get saved anyway. That's why it works for me. There's always a reason to procrastinate saving. With it arranged in advance, you won't postpone; money will be locked away when you get the deposit advice.

However, discipline is required to leave it alone and watch the balance rise. If you withdraw when your favorite band comes to town, or for Aunt Betty's birthday, it will be a pointless exercise.

Save it and forget it. As a financial coach, I help clients to get on a budget and save at least $1000 cash for a basic cushion. A written plan will let you build a savings category and grow it over time. Since a coach is an objective third party, I can usually see ways to improve with money the client may overlook.

After you have $1000, keep saving until you have three months of your income set aside, because a major car repair could wipe out $1000 in a day. This will take time, but at least move toward the goal.

When I first heard the suggestion, it seemed impossible, so I didn't attempt it. Why bother? And I was correct since I didn't believe I could do it. You will never accomplish what you don't believe you can. Two words came to me: "Why Not?"

I convinced myself it *was* possible to save three months wages, then I did it. You can too. It took longer than I hoped but I got there. It's better to take twice as long to reach a goal, than to never set one, and then not hit it.

I've known people with good, stable incomes, that had to scramble financially when an injury or sickness appeared unexpectedly. And those things are always unexpected. They had to plunge in credit card debt, borrow from relatives and damage their creditworthiness to stay afloat. This is avoidable with a reliable income. Don't spend all of it! Set a little aside. You will thank yourself later. I promise.

For starters, work towards $1000. You'll be surprised at the sense of independence savings will bring. You will find creative ways to save if you look hard, be honest with yourself and they will appear. Enjoy the rewards of taking action to improve your life and build a moneyhouse to be proud of.

- Use a quality bank account to manage your assets.
- Become a saver!
- Set Goals. Devise ways to reach them.

Profile #3
RE-ARRANGED PRIORITIES

Carol and Doug are married and in their early thirties. They're employed full time with two kids they adore, working opposite shifts so the other can stay with the children.

This arrangement works for awhile, but Carol realizes her time is better spent with her family than earning a paycheck. She hates missing the daily life moments children bring. They grow up fast and change a little each day. Staying home felt impossible since the family relied on her income.

The couple reviewed every dollar in the budget several times, then took a leap of faith. Carol cut her hours to part-time. It wasn't ideal but a step in the right direction.

The following months were difficult. The income reduction brought financial strain neither expected. However, improvement of their home life made them determined to make it work. The kids loved Mom being home. It was more peaceful for them without traveling to work, transferring to the other parent, and driving home as often.

Although Carol was the career type, family was a

higher call to answer. The decision to struggle financially would impact the next generation. Fulfilling days at home made shuffling paper for the county feel pointless. This was a necessary change, regardless of the money pressure.

Together they reevaluated each dollar and priorities. They cut coupons, and changed how they shopped. Ready to eat food is expensive. Carol cooked from scratch, healthier as well as cheaper.

Doug sold a fishing boat and paid down debt to keep dollars in the budget. The family's contentedness was a priority over fishing, which only happened once a month anyway.

Fun changed as well. The family discovered backyard campfires. Carol played her guitar as they roasted marshmallows. These simple pleasures were as satisfying as ones that used to break the bank. Instead of restaurants, they enjoyed picnics in the park. In place of movies, storytelling at the library. Date nights were less flashy, but more frequent. Money was tight but quality of life thrived.

People define success as having what you want. This family is as successful as they come.

Sometimes we're in lockstep with the crowd, until we realize they aren't very content or happy. It's good to evaluate the satisfaction (or lack of it) our efforts bring, and have the courage to make the unpopular decision to pursue the road less travelled.

Courage and good money skills gave Doug and Carol the family life they always desired.

Hey there!

This is Dave, I'm the author.

I hope you're getting some useful insights from the book so far. I wanted to ask a favor. It would mean a lot to me if you would leave a review on Amazon. Authors live and die by reviews, and yours would be a tremendous help.

Thank you so much!

CHAPTER IV
Break the Chains to attain Freedom

A man in debt is a man in chains.
— *James Lendall Basford*

DUMP THE DEBT

You and I live during an unusual time in history. Events are occurring previous generations never witnessed. During the financial crisis of 2008 -2009, the federal government poured billions of dollars down a black hole with little improvement to our economy; borrowed money that still needs to be repaid.

Abroad, nations stood on the brink of financial collapse while citizens protested any measure to prevent it. Nations worried if a neighboring country would default, their own economy would suffer since that country owed them money.

In this global economy, we are linked to each other like mountain climbers. Everyone gets nervous when they hear distressing cries from climbers above and see them digging their fingernails into the crevices to hang on.

The whole world is addicted to spending money they don't have. It's a matter of time before it comes due and becomes their ruin. It isn't much different individually; just smaller numbers.

According to Bloomberg, Americans owed $936 billion in credit card and revolving debt. MarketWatch says the average debt of college graduates is $35,051. 76% of college students hold credit cards. It's been a growing trend for some time.

In 1968, total credit card debt was $8 billion. The Federal Reserve says it will reach one trillion dollars by 2016. That is one thousand piles of money, each one being a billion dollars. This is irresponsibility on steroids. A small problem like an annoying squirrel stealing bird seed has morphed into King Kong kicking over police cars.

There's an even higher cost we pay. What's not

shown on the credit card statement are divorces being filed because of endless money fights. Financial stress has a ripple effect. We can't be the happy, contented and productive people God meant us to be if we're plagued by fear and anxiety. Debt steals our joy.

Kids are victims as well. They suffer when both parents must work. They eyewitness the dissention and learn from us how to manage money. For some, that is frightening indeed. Are we modeling a lifestyle that will bring the same stress and bondage to our kids?

We mentioned the "Greatest Generation" in the last chapter. The people who fought and won World War II rarely had two incomes, but had enough because they were wise. They didn't need to own everything they saw. In that era, one had sympathy for a neighbor who had to borrow money. It meant things weren't going well for them. A bank note was a crutch to make due until the person was able to stand alone again. The nation and individual families fared much better with that mindset. While we have advanced far beyond the norms of that era, we should preserve the financial common sense prevalent in their day. Our smartphones and digital music may be superior to the large, wall mounted telephones and scratchy vinyl records but they have us beat with a straightforward approach to money and the resulting lack of anxiety.

Our generation feels successful because of a nice car they need a huge loan to drive. Our perspectives have become carnival mirrors that reflect the opposite of reality. We pity a person with an older car because they must be too poor to afford a monthly payment. We instead should admire them for banking what others lose in depreciation. Spare the sympathy and imitate the wisdom.

At the same time, we admire the driver of a beautiful car because . . . Why? Because he qualified for the loan, committed the next seven years of his income? Is that all we need for admiration, the ability to plunge into debt, while ignoring interest paid and depreciation?

It's time we said "Enough already!" We may not be able to stop the foolishness in Washington, DC, but we can get our own houses in order. We might recognize the salesman and the lender benefit much more from our "status symbol" than we do.

Americans need to break up with debt. What I mean is to stop believing the so-called experts who are comfortable with debt. It's a common practice to borrow money. Corporations, the Federal Government and all the "smart" people in the world lose no sleep over rising debt. After all, it's the way things are done. Companies aren't up to their neck in debt, they are "leveraged." As though a cool term makes the financial situation any different.

Well, the experts are dead wrong. Owning money is better than owing any day. Freedom from debt gives you options; you are more secure if your future earnings aren't already spent. We commit a grave error by assuming experts are correct because they wear the label "expert". Suppose what they say flies in the face of common sense? What if the results of their advice are disastrous? Will we still listen because someone called them an expert?

It's high time that Americans quit following these pied pipers over the cliff. We don't have a money printing press so we can't follow the example of the Government. You have a sound mind, trust your common sense and follow your instincts.

DREAM AND VISUALIZE

How would life look if the only money you owed was for utilities and cable service you used last month? If you had no car payment, owed nothing for your home, and the credit card balance was zero, how would it change the way you approach tomorrow? What activities could you consider that isn't even in the realm of possibility now? Maybe you could travel to places you've only dreamed of, live in the home you never thought possible, or get your degree? Perhaps you could help drill wells or send food to impoverished nations. Marketers hope you never discover the options you have if you say no to their offers.

This is completely possible, and liberating. People are dumping their debt every day and discover a whole new outlook on life. This may seem radical and a little odd to most Americans, but then, the average American is saddled with debt he'll never pay off. So what if you look like an oddball to that guy? He'll just be struggling to stay afloat his whole life. Why crave his admiration? Americans like impressing people we don't know.

We want to look like a successful, on top of the world kind of person to . . . whom? The person beside you at the red light, admiring your car? The neighbor whose name you don't know? The stranger who sees you walking from the home you struggle to pay for? Think differently. Think above the crowd. Have a vision! What if you drove an older car not as impressive to the dude next to you at the light? What if, instead of a car payment, you invested in a 401K, or a growth stock mutual fund that would let you retire a millionaire, or at least years sooner than the guy with the Corvette beside you?

A positive of debt is you can have something now you can't really afford, which stops being a positive when the payment comes due. The benefit is short-lived. As mature adults, we raise our self-esteem by planning for what we want, and being patient for it. Self denial reminds us we're not spoiled children, but rather the decider of our destinies.

It *is* possible to live without debt. Believe that. People did it for years before this well-marketed, "buy it now" disease surged in popularity.

DROWNING IN DEBT

What if you are over your head in debt, what then? Can you turn the situation around? ABSOLUTELY!

Step One: This is the most important one, and it won't cost a thin dime. Make the crucial decision to get out of debt, and begin to change your mindset and habits. Debt is not a money problem. It is a habit problem. Money will go wherever you send it. It's just doing its job and obeying orders. The problem lies in the operator. This isn't an insult; it's truth. A hundred dollars will do the same for me as for you. The mission we send it on makes the difference. I may pay for a nice dinner I charged to a credit card last year, and you may invest in a mutual fund that may grow into a few thousand dollars by retirement. The choice is yours. This is exciting if you make the right choice. Refuse to go any lower into the hole you may find yourself in.

Step Two: The next step should be to begin to navigate out of the wilderness. What might that look like? Track your expenditures, and work out a money plan to cover all expenses for the month without using debt. Take time to get it right. To get affairs in order, know what you have and where it goes. Be patient. Be diligent.

Okay. Let's assume you broke up with debt and sent the slave-driver off to beat up someone else. You have a written plan and are sticking to it pretty well. The problem is, you still owe a lot of money and very little to spare. This is a lousy spot. You are doing the work but waiting for the rewards promised. All blood, sweat and tears without payday ever coming. This can start to change now.

Step 3: Devise a plan and move into attack mode. Become determined and assault the debts you still owe. Tear the leeches off one by one. Find some money to make each one go away. But how?

Everyone's situation is different of course, but similar nonetheless. Sell some of the junk in your attic or garage (Hello Craigslist or Offer Up). It could mean selling a car or a boat to get back on your feet. For some, this could be a double-edged approach. Besides being rid of a monthly payment, if you have equity, it may be a cash surplus as well.

Lifestyle changes may be all that's necessary to pull out of the ditch and get on the road. In addition to tobacco, lunches and coffee being a great place to find money in a tight plan, let's look at other possibilities. Some situations may demand some extra work. A part-time job may be beneath your dignity. It was beneath mine too when I had one. But, humility is a virtue. To raise your standard of living in the long run, your pride may take a hit in the short term. You'll survive, I did. You're reading this because you desire a better life. A side gig will help you get there. The financial boost that derives from working a few nights a week may be surprising.

Nothing is accomplished without a level of sacrifice. To achieve a mountaintop view, you must scratch, climb and sweat before you reach it.

If an extra job is impossible, find something you no longer need, and sell it. You may be a clotheshorse. Selling clothing at a consignment shop could be a small windfall. Go through your storage space and resist the hoarding tendency. As in the other scenarios, it carries fringe benefits. Besides finding cash for your plan, you may also reduce clutter in the garage or discover your closet is larger than you remember it.

Be creative and search diligently for ways to free up money and you will find them. As you do, the extra should go directly to paying down debt.

One of my heroes is Dave Ramsey. He is host of

the Dave Ramsey Show, heard across America. I believe he has the best plan for paying off debt. Dave teaches about the "Debt Snowball." Make a list of all the debts you owe, smallest to largest. You begin to pay down extra money on the smallest debt until it's paid. Then take the minimum payment you used to make on the one paid off, and pay it on the next one above (along with its regular minimum payment). There is great wisdom in this. First, paying down to zero and eliminating a monthly payment is encouraging. This gives you a victory or two early in the battle to celebrate. And celebrating is FUN! Here's an example:

	CREDITOR	AMOUNT OWED	MINIMUM PAYMENT	INTEREST RATE
1	Mom and Dad	$250	$20	0%
2	Ball and Chain Finance	$430	$20	18%
3	Bondage Credit Card	$1327	$50	16%
4	Sellitback Corp (Home Equity)	$4600	$185	4.5%
5	Crooks R Us (Auto Loan)	$5400	$325	3.2%

6	1st National Bank (Mortgage)	$86,300	$735	5.0%

Notice the debts are listed from smallest to largest (amounts owed). The method for getting out of the dark hole and into the sunlight of freedom, starts with finding extra money for debt #1. Simply continue to pay all the regular amounts on all debts. But find, create or produce extra money to pay off the smallest debt faster. Notice that debt #1 charges no interest. Pay it off first anyway. Ignore interest rates. The payment itself is more substantial. Pay down the smallest amount owed.

Once Mom and Dad are paid off, take the amount you once paid them, and combine it with the regular minimum payment to the #2 debtor (Ball and Chain Finance). This will double the payment to that debt. Any extra paid will bring the balance down even quicker.

You have one less debt to pay now, and have DOUBLED the payment on #2 debt. Once #2 is eliminated, take the payments from #1 and 2, and add it to #3 along with its regular amount. This is the formula to get completely free of debt. It's that simple, but not fast. This does require patience and takes time.

But it's worth it. Continuing with the same formula, you will get them all paid off. All of those former minimum payments now belong to you. They are owed to no one.

To reach these goals, keep your eye on the goal of a debt-free life. Know that it's possible to do and envision yourself doing it.

Remember to ignore interest rates. It may seem counter-intuitive, but it frees cash up to pay more than the minimum payment on the next debt. The pace accelerates as you pack the former minimum payments into your snowball to pay off the next debt on the list. If I had a better plan, I would use it. But this one works great. So I'll refrain from tampering with a perfect model. You can see more at www.daveramsey.com.

CREDIT CARDS

You may be wondering about credit cards. Should I have one? Is there life without one? To begin with, there is more danger than benefit. Nearly every business in America issues their own credit card they want you to have. I held several when I thought more like the average person. One for the gas station that I always used (I saved 2c per gallon too), one from my favorite department store, a home improvement store and a few others I can't recall.

I closed them all years ago. It became a juggling act, paying each on time, and remembering which had a balance and which didn't. It was insanity.

At the beginning, these creditors seemed like great people to do business with. I quickly learned that mercy and forgiveness was not their strong suit. If I was two days late on a $20.00 payment, the late charge could be $25 or more.

Credit card companies earn profits from late fees or exceeding your limit. Credit is touted as a wonderful convenience, but in reality, everyone missteps eventually. When it happens, they will charge outrageous fees for an innocent oversight. I promise.

I now hold only one major card, used primarily for online purchases. I've had my identity stolen several times and don't like my debit card number floating in cyberspace. While most debit cards hold the same fraud protection as credit cards, it may take seven to fourteen days to have the funds returned. It's easy to live without a credit card for two weeks, but much trickier if it's all the money in my bank account.

I never pay interest because I pay it off immediately.

Credit cards possess a subtle danger the companies fail to warn about, similar to financial dynamite. Highway developers and mining companies use explosives often. It is a valuable, time saving tool, but if mishandled in any way, it is ugly and potentially deadly.

Credit is the same. No one intends to get careless with it. When it happens, any memory of convenience is erased, and being hounded by a collector is not fun.

The great entertainer P.T. Barnum once said "Money is in some respects life's fire: It is a very excellent servant, but a terrible master." That truth is never more clear than when a collection agency is unleashed on your trail. These people are paid to make your life hellish. But if the balance is paid when the bill comes, it remains a "servant."

But often it's not, and the balance carries over until next month. A problem may arise and the balance due increases just a little bit. Not much, though. Still nothing to worry about. "I'll pay it off this time for sure." The next bill cycle may have its own surprise, which prevents it from being fully paid.

We've all heard of folks with ten or twenty thousand dollars in credit card debt. None of those people acquired the card with the intent of plunging hopelessly over their head. It happens slowly and is barely perceptible.

In time, it becomes a crisis. Like a river to an inexperienced swimmer, credit looks easy, so they jump in! He soon learns the water is deeper than expected, and the current is much stronger than it looked. He tires, as the shore drifts farther away. Extreme caution should be used with credit. It can be terrifying very quickly.

Paying with cash in hand is the safest route. It's impossible to overspend with cash. Purchases made with cash never have a late fee. Also, cash buyers are likely to spend less. Studies have shown that consumers may spend 5 – 10% more when a credit card is used. Credit users show less restraint, because the pain isn't immediate. Conversely, when one must count out the bills, and are instantly poorer, we tend to be more frugal. Using cash saves you cash.

- Avoid debt like the plague it is. If you're in debt, GET OUT NOW!
- Possess a healthy fear of credit cards. They're flat snakes without fangs.

Profile #4
MISSED OPPORTUNITIES

At first glance, these profiles may not seem directly related to money. But decisions overlap and touch other areas, including our finances.

Brent is eighteen years old and about to graduate high school. With excellent grades, his family encouraged him to apply for scholarships. Although tedious and time consuming, it paid off. An excellent college nearby awarded Brent a full scholarship, allowing him to commute and save housing costs too. His proud parents were the envy of others applying for student loans or draining their savings.

But Brent wasn't excited. The school had a reputation for academic excellence, but not for fun. It was a Catholic institution with a rich history; burning candles, chapels and statues of saints conveyed a religious, old feeling. These things were noticeably absent from *his* vision of college. None of his friends would be attending.

Ignoring his parents' pleas, Brent decided to attend a university a hundred twenty miles from home. Commuting would be impossible but his buds were there. Without a scholarship, he had to apply for financial aid. The education gave him the same degree and career he would've gotten from the Catholic school, but at a much higher cost.

A decade later, Brent is reminded monthly of his poor decision when he makes a payment on his student loan. Unfortunately, he lost touch with his college friends who were so important at the time.
Part two is about another high school graduate. Dave grew up in Pennsylvania but the family moved to Florida after his father's death. Tenth grade brought many sudden changes, but Dave landed jobs and made friends during his high school years.

Now it was decision time. Upon graduation, he had to choose between returning to Pennsylvania with his mom, or staying in Florida on his own. While pondering the choice a friend's dad offered him a job with his company. The position would train him in every aspect of the heating and air conditioning business. The owner was a good honest man and really liked Dave. With no money for college, it was an amazing career opportunity.

I'd love to report he jumped on the chance with both feet. He didn't. In fact, he barely considered the offer. Being homesick and afraid of the unfamiliar, Dave returned to dismal prospects in familiar

Pennsylvania and never found another opportunity like the one he passed up.

He loved Florida, so he returned twenty four years later with his family to make up for lost time. He spent most of the intervening years in a boring, unfulfilling job that left his family struggling financially.

We all make decisions that affect the outcome of our lives. They have varying degrees of consequence, but choices matter. It's important to consider an option even if it's not your first pick. We often pass up a perfect solution simply because it wasn't on the original list of considerations.

It's great to say "Let me think about it" before jumping directly to "No." At times the treasure chest of gold is disguised as a bucket of sand and we miss it for lack of perspective. Consider the second or third alternatives as well. They may be the grand prize.

CHAPTER V
How to Maintain Accounts

There are no shortcuts to anyplace worth going

— Beverly Sills

THE CHECKING ACCOUNT

Whenever you create something of value, there is a maintenance factor necessary to preserve what you've worked for. In a neighborhood, the homeowner needs to mow the lawn, pull weeds and make repairs to keep the value up and prevent a hostile mob of neighbors. You don't want to be the one with a '77 Camaro on blocks and a refrigerator on the back porch.

It's the same with your moneyhouse. Routine upkeep insures it will continue to serve you well and increase in value.

It's time to introduce another skill to drive the momentum forward. Many people don't reconcile their accounts monthly, because they don't see the need or never learned how. The statements can be convoluted and intimidating. We will unpack it one piece at a time, and dispel the boogeyman aspect of it.

Feel free to bypass this chapter if it doesn't apply. But it will be helpful for many.

Why bother with this? How will balancing my account help me gain control of my money?

With online banking, some say it's unnecessary to reconcile because you can cross the transactions off as they clear the bank and find the new balance. This is true in two scenarios.

The first is if you have six transactions per month and the second if you want a new boring hobby tracking everything online. Neither one works for me.

Also, the bank may have a lag time of a few days, even for electronic transactions. If you operate using the account balance online, it will seldom be accurate due to the lag time, and you could potentially overdraw.

Remember, contentment is the goal. Like having a budget, balancing (or reconciling) the checking account is to eliminate surprises. Accidentally running out of money is expensive. Besides making up the shortfall, you'll be charged fees by your bank and the retailer where the transaction occurred.

For a small mistake, you could shell out $50 to $75, assuming only one check or transaction was returned. This is a great incentive to keep your numbers as straight as possible. Keep in mind you can overdraw your account with a debit card also. Reconciling the account monthly insures you and the bank are on the same page and agree how much money is in the account.

Don't believe the lie that accuracy with numbers eliminates the need for reconciling. When it comes to numbers, I'm borderline obsessive-compulsive and drive my poor wife crazy. Even so, if there isn't a mistake for two months in a row, I break out the good stuff and celebrate. At least I will when it happens. There are too many opportunities for errors.

Maintaining your account gives you a sense of control; it tames the belligerent master into an obedient, polite servant. Without unexpected charges, you control *all* of your money. Since you've earned it, you should decide where it goes, not bank fees.

Note: Checks are becoming increasingly obsolete in our electronic age, but since they're still in use, we'll discuss checks to complete the body of knowledge. Even if you don't write checks, you'll still reconcile the account like this.

First, we want to understand the checking statement. Some are straightforward. Others are more complicated. Spend time to review it carefully until it makes sense. If you have questions, ask your bank representative.

It's important that you learn to navigate through all of it. Each statement is categorized into several different sections. Taken one at a time, it isn't hard to decipher.

THE BALANCE SECTION

The first section will be the Balance section which shows your account balance for the beginning of the period, balance at the end of the same period; and an average daily balance (which is unnecessary for most of us). If you have several accounts with the same institution, it will probably show the balance of all accounts here.

DEPOSITS AND CREDITS

This section lists all the deposits for the month, including date and amount. They could be listed as credits or deposits. They mean the same thing, funds placed into your account to raise the balance: a direct deposited paycheck, money (cash, checks or money orders) you carry into a teller or money transferred from a savings account.

CHECKS

CHECKS section shows each check processed, the amount and date it cleared. When a check clears, it means it was presented to the bank for payment, and funds paid to the person or entity the check was written to.

MISCELLANEOUS DEBITS

The next section may be called various names but it is usually referred to as Miscellaneous Debits. Just as credits and deposits go in and raise the balance, debits and withdrawals show money leaving the account and lower the balance.

This includes checks, ATM withdrawals, debit card purchases, automatic recurring withdrawals you have set up, or taking cash at the teller window. Any payout is listed. If you have a savings account, it will be in a separate section. The sequence and titles of each may vary, but these are the basic statement components.

HOW TO RECONCILE THE BANK'S NUMBERS WITH YOUR NUMBERS

Note; many statements have instructions on the back explaining how to reconcile the account. I haven't found them "user friendly." But if yours makes sense, use it or try this way. Also, some banking software will do this automatically. But it is worth knowing how to do manually so you completely understand the process. Children are still taught math even though a calculator will achieve the end result. Likewise with the budget. If you scratch it out with a pen and paper it's more personal to you than with an electronic spreadsheet and it feels exclusive to your situation.

First, verify the deposits for the month. In other words, make sure the bank has the exact same deposit amounts you entered in the register or wherever you record transactions to track the money. (The register is the gray and white lined booklet that slides in above the checks.) The register should show checks written, deposits made, debit card purchases, ATM withdrawals, automatic payments and anything else that occurs to affect the account balance. Many people never bother recording any account transactions. They may periodically check online but don't record the daily changes. There's no judgement but if you're in that group, I would encourage you to begin. It may feel a bit tedious at first but it's necessary to gain the control you want in order to be efficient. This is the Money Record. It looks like this:

Check no.	Date	Transaction Description	Amount	Deposit	Balance
1827	8-2	Jerry's Grocery	46.27		287.34
ATM	8-4	1st National	40.00		247.34
online	8-5	Utilities Co.	55.36		191.98
Deposit	8-7	Acme Co.	XXXX	627.67	819.65
1828	8-2	Sam's Garage	54.18		765.47
TFR	8-12	Transfer to Savings	75.00		690.47

For example, the bank may show a deposit for $285.00 on the 10th of the month. Put a check mark beside that deposit and one beside the amount on the bank statement. Be certain the two records (your register and their statement) agree. If there is a discrepancy, figure out which transaction amount is correct and adjust the incorrect one. We mark it with a check to know the ground we already covered. Anything marked with a check is verified and done, you can move on.

My experience has been most blunders are my fault. Banks make mistakes, but it's rare.

Financial institutions are pretty good at what they do.

If you are paid the same amount each pay period, don't assume you were paid the usual amount. Verify the deposit. Assumptions leave the back door open for mistakes and surprises to enter. Surprises cause chaos. Attention to details eliminates it. Double check your numbers.

With deposits verified and mistakes corrected, move to the list of checks paid from your account, numerically sequenced. Verify each check amount as you did for the deposit section. (If you never write checks, this will be informational only). Go slow and be detail oriented. A common mistake is transposition, which is a fancy word for swapping or transposing the digits.

For example, you may write a check for $32.69 but you enter $32.96 in your register. It's not a large amount but will throw the numbers off. Note: If the discrepancy amount is divisible by nine, it may be a transposition error.

This is one of the rewards to reconciling the account every month. A small mistake is easily fixed when caught early, but a few errors per month could accumulate into a large problem if left unchecked. Getting back on track will be untangling a fishing reel beyond hope.

Be aware of the closing date on your statement. This is the cutoff date; the last day of business for the statement. Most banks use the calendar month while others use some other date. It's not important as long as you know the date. A missing transaction on your statement may have occurred after the close date and will appear on next month's business.

An asterisk beside check numbers indicates that the sequence was broken. For example, suppose the list shows checks #821, #822 and #825. If #825 is marked with an asterisk, this means checks numbered 823 and 824 haven't yet arrived at the bank. The missing checks may have been written near the cut off date. They are "outstanding." It's not to say they're more gifted or wonderful than other checks, only they're out there and will reach the bank soon. When verifying amounts, make a list of outstanding ones. They affect the ending balance.

Note: If you write a check, it will be processed electronically and show as an electronic or debit transaction, and may not be in the check lineup. Mark each check matching the statement and your register, just as in the deposit section. Correct errors. Each check mark indicates you are doing things right. Each check mark puts you closer to a reconciled account.

ELECTRONIC TRANSACTIONS

Verify amounts in the electronic debits section. All ATM withdrawals, debit card purchases and checks processed electronically will be listed by date in this section. Note: Dating each transaction in the register will speed this process and reduce searching. The goal is to confirm the bank has done the same additions and subtractions that you have.

Sometimes a legibility problem causes trouble, or forgetting to enter a transaction. I have searched several weeks of transactions to locate the cause of discrepancy. One wrong keypunch on the calculator and everything that follows is wrong.

With everything verified, make two columns. One side will be "The Bank", the other side "Me", or "My Numbers." The bank side begins with the Ending Balance amount. Subtract any outstanding checks from their balance. We remove those amounts because they're already deducted in your register (and will be from theirs when they arrive at the bank for payment).

Next, find *your* ending balance. Add or subtract the verified transactions to arrive at the account balance according to your figures. Remember, gaps between check marked items are normal. The unchecked ones will be on next month's statement.

This will give you your ending balance. Compare it to the bank's ending balance. If the two amounts match, the account is successfully reconciled.

In a nutshell, reconciling the account is simply making sure the bank agrees you have "X" amount of money at the close of a certain day of the month. It's like communication in a strong relationship. It eliminates assumptions and verifies both parties are operating on the same information.

BALANCE TOO LOW?

What if the balances don't match? What then? Don't panic. It's a matter of figuring out why. Let's assume that the bank's ending balance is higher than your balance. For example, the bank says you have $803.00 but according to your register, you have only $746.00. This would indicate you deducted money from your balance that perhaps the bank has not yet processed.

Confirm all outstanding items are deducted from the bank's ending balance. Verify an item wasn't deducted twice in your records. Be sure your arithmetic is accurate. It could be you deducted a charge the bank hasn't charged yet (for checks ordered for example).

Any of these scenarios would make their balance higher than yours.

BALANCE TOO HIGH?

But what if the opposite is true? Maybe your balance is higher than the bank's. This is a little more disturbing since you've been operating under the delusion you have more money than you actually do. *How* disturbing depends on the size of the gap.

In this case, the bank deducted something you did not. Or they didn't add something you did.

Maybe you entered a deposit in your register but never made it to the bank to actually deposit the money. (Good intentions without follow up, I'm a member of that club too.) There may have been a charge you were unaware of, or perhaps a deposit wasn't properly credited to the account.

If the last statement balanced correctly, the answer to the riddle is somewhere on the statement or register. Search line by line until the discrepancy is found.

CELEBRATE!

Resist feeling overwhelmed. You've got this! Fear not. Soon reconciling the account will be second nature and you'll be glad you hung in there. Anything new carries a level of angst at the beginning.

It's a good idea to maintain your finances with enough time to complete the whole process. Play relaxing music if it helps, but remove anxiety from the process.

You'll be required to manage money until your last day on the planet. Make friends with it and decide to be great at it. Have your act together instead of looking like you do. The next step is to celebrate. You've added to your list of skills. Congratulations!

ADDITIONAL THOUGHTS

As attention to details grows, consider expanding this skill to other areas. For example, do you really know what each line of your power bill or credit card statement means? Have you ever called them to question a charge? You should. It's your money they are asking for.

If a stranger demanded $3.78 without explanation, you probably wouldn't pay it. But you may be doing it with your cell phone carrier or cable provider.

If an item is unclear on a bill, ask for an explanation and request the charge be waived. They often comply. If not, mention several companies would love you as a customer with your great payment history. They may put you on hold, and return with good news.

I don't want to beat these companies up, so I'll pay for requested services. But it's a business transaction, and I won't pay for what I haven't asked for. You shouldn't either. Ask, clarify and understand the whole bill.

If you forget to cancel a trial promotion you've decided against, they will charge you FOREVER (until you stop it).

The point is to scrutinize every dollar. Leave no stone unturned. A fresh look at something you've seen many times reveals surprises. Assume nothing and re-evaluate everything.

- Reconcile your accounts monthly to keep the numbers accurate
- Pay attention to the details of your bills and statements.

Profile #5
WHEN THE INCOME STOPS

Cassie and Bryce have been married for four years. Bryce cooks for a restaurant but music is his passion. He gives lessons part time at a local charter school.

When Cassie graduated college with a teaching degree, she was fortunate enough to land a position at the same school where her husband taught. They love their kids and the elementary so much, eventually both became full time educators.

While education offers many rewards, like helping young people succeed and building relationships, there's a downside. The drawback is when the school year ends so does the income.

Many teachers were married to people who worked year round, so summer break didn't impact their finances as much. But Bryce and Cassie had a unique challenge. Both incomes ended.

Few employers want to hire if they know you'll quit in less than three months. Most temporary positions are filled by college students who return each summer.

The couple's first year was the hardest. They waited too long to seek employment and paid the price with a few lean months, and vowed to begin the search earlier to be ready next time around.

Bryce's grandfather visited near the end of that first rough summer. Bryce was eager to hear Grandpa's insight. The old man grew up during the Great Depression, giving him a rare perspective and wisdom.

During the visit, the couple related the predicament they had.

Grandpa listened carefully and then said "You know, over the years I've learned there are many types and flavors of bad situations. There is the kind we cause ourselves by poor judgement, or plain stupid choices. Those can be avoided with experience.

"Then there is the kind that we have no control over, and often can't see coming. It blindsides us without so much as a warning. It can knock us off our feet and leave us wondering where it came from. Those are tough customers.

"Another type of crisis is the one that sends warning signs a long way off. It sounds a little louder as it gets closer. You're never sure *exactly* when it will show up, but it will. It's the inevitable problem we should all be ready for, but we procrastinate hoping it's farther away."

"Then there is your kind. It's the best type of crisis to have." Grandpa leaned back in his chair.

The couple exchanged glances, hoping the other had a clue. "Why is it the best type of crisis to have?" Bryce asked.

"Well it's obvious. It's the best type of problem because you know exactly when it will occur. You also know how long the situation will last, to the very day! An emergency is something that crops up unexpectedly. It isn't much of an emergency if you can have a countdown almost a year in advance." He smiled.

Grandpa stroked his graying beard. "What if you prepared for what was coming and set aside, say, ten percent of your income into a special account? If you do it for ten months while school is in session, you have one month salary saved. If you both saved, you will have replaced one income for the summer. Granted, you'd have to watch expenses since it's still a reduction, but it's some breathing room you don't have now."

There was a pause as they digested the resourceful idea.

"I'm a little embarrassed something so obvious

didn't occur to us." Cassie admitted. "It's a great idea."

"It sure is. But I was just thinking if we could save a little more, we wouldn't have to work *any* temporary jobs. We would have two months each year to do what we want. We could take month long camping trips. We could drive across the country at our leisure, or visit family." Bryce looked at his wife, "You've been wanting to plant a garden Cassie."

Grandpa sighed. "That's what advance planning does. It gives you options."

The teachers in this profile are unique. Summers off would be out of reach for most. But the primary lesson is routinely saving money prevents desperation and being forced to choose between lousy options. Difficulties arise, expected or not.

The greater counsel is being prepared puts you in command of the situation. You aren't being being led around like a birthday pony by the circumstances, forced into a poor choice due to lack of funds. Save money. Be the one in the Director's chair with the megaphone shouting how it will go.

When we make financial decisions like everyone else, we'll find ourselves in the same tough spots.

Different thinking leads to lifestyles envied by the crowd. Craft a vision for an exceptional life.

CHAPTER VI
Big Ticket Items

The only reason a great many American families don't own an elephant is that they have never been offered an elephant for a dollar down and easy weekly payments.

— Mad Magazine

We've covered basic topics concerning finances, budgets, debt reduction and account maintenance. Since money is complex and touches everything, it pays to educate yourself before making large purchases. Some spend more time planning a great vacation or a party than their personal finances. Here's a few thoughts to ponder.

HOUSES

A home is the biggest investment you'll ever make. There are pitfalls to avoid when buying your largest asset.

One mistake to avoid is the ARM. It stands for Adjustable Rate Mortgage (also called a Variable Rate Mortgage). ARMs are attractive because of the initially lower rate, tied to an economic index, making the payment more affordable. After a period of time, the interest may rise or fall with the movement of the index.

The lender usually chooses the index. Some offer annual caps and lifetime caps. For example, let's say it's a 5/1 ARM. This means it operates as a fixed rate loan for the first five years. After that, the rate is adjusted once per year. The cap prevents a large hike in one period. There are endless variations and combinations of options.

While an ARM costs less during the first few years, it has disadvantages. How well versed is the average homebuyer in the rise or fall of economic indexes? Can they predict what the rate will be three years in the future? Even if you're current with market trends, your mortgage payment is linked to an uncontrollable force. What drives the index higher? A Middle East crisis? Consumer confidence? Treasury notes? The buyer has no control over these influences.

ARMs became popular in a high interest environment. It was the only way homebuyers could get a home. They make less sense when the rates are lower. The savings aren't there to justify the risk. Lenders argue that ARMs are great because most people will sell the house before the rate adjusts. Perhaps. What if they can't sell, or decide not to?

The ARM is a bad idea simply because you are building uncertainty into your future. The goal is contentment in your finances. An adjustable rate plants seeds of chaos that may sprout when you're least prepared. People have lost homes because the rate adjustment made the payment unaffordable.

A fixed rate may be a higher interest rate initially, but payments remain constant. Predictability is priceless in finances. Don't sell stability for a teaser rate up front.

HELOCS

Another common instrument marketed well is the HELOC. It stands for Home Equity Line Of Credit. The attraction of home ownership is that you will eventually own something worth having. It'll be yours after the last payment. What a great goal.

But with the advent of the HELOC, the family home has become a large ATM. It's common to borrow against it for cars or vacations. This is poor financial logic. When a homeowner does this, they are financing a ten day cruise for the next 15 to 20 years. MEGA "Bad Idea".

We've discussed earlier generations. Their common sense and homespun wisdom would never let them consider this. The goal is to own the home, not continuously sell it back to the bank.

You may argue, "times have changed." It's true, they have. But not every change is good. By every standard you can measure, that generation was more successful. Generally, they saved well, carried little debt and lived in homes that were paid for. Success should be imitated regardless of the era.

STAY IN DEBT OR DEBT FREE?

There's bad information being given about the mortgage deduction. Some money gurus will advise you not to pay off your mortgage in order to keep the tax deduction. This is a sophisticated trick experts use to shrink your tax bill. The only benefit is less taxable income may keep you in a lower tax bracket.

But for most, this philosophy will have them paying *many* thousands in interest to prevent paying a *few* thousand in taxes. It's faulty logic. The "experts" will advise to stay in debt in order to pay less to the IRS. This is nonsense. If you pay $12000 in mortgage interest to the bank, to be able to send $4000 less in taxes to the government, you still have less money. The bankers recommend this for obvious reasons. They enjoy your thousands of dollars in interest paid to them each year. Pay off your home if you're able, and you own an asset free and clear. The satisfaction and security is more valuable than a deduction. Own your home. It's great!

PAY TWICE

One way to pay your mortgage off sooner is the biweekly payment. If you can arrange it, you pay the lender every two weeks instead of once a month. The amount is the regular payment cut in half, but over the course of one year, you will make an extra payment because of the months that have an extra week. By year's end, you have made thirteen payments instead of twelve. Over the life of the mortgage, you pay it down quicker, yet the amount you pay each month is the same. Since the mortgage is paid more often, interest is reduced because the principal drops faster. With the additional payment, more goes to the loan balance and less to interest. It's a win-win.

Another technique to drop the balance even faster is to make an extra payment in January. When you do, you are paying interest on a lower amount for the remainder of the year. Similar to the bi-weekly idea, this also lowers the balance faster. The results are impressive over the life of the mortgage.

If that isn't possible, throw a few extra dollars onto each payment. If the payment is $852, round it up to $860 or more. It isn't a large amount, but still a movement in the right direction.

BUY WHAT YOU CAN AFFORD

The last advice for home buying is to learn from recent history. Our economy took a huge hit in 2008 after politicians pressured lenders to reduce mortgage standards in order to brag about high rates of home ownership. Banks complied and required little documentation or income verification, then sold the sub prime loans to investors.

When the economy slowed, financially unprepared people lost their homes in droves (many were Adjustable Rate Mortgages). This precipitated the housing crash. The bankers who knew better assisted the disaster, along with the politicians who promoted this false, feel good propaganda.

The point is it's a bad idea to buy before you're ready. The home will be a burden instead of the benefit you hoped for. As a homeowner, you're responsible for all repairs and maintenance. And if the monthly payment keeps you broke, the needed repairs can't be made. Be patient. Become a homeowner when you can truly afford it. Remember the higher the down payment, the lower the monthly payment will be, which is further incentive to save.

When you do buy, be aware lenders will

generally approve more home than you can practically afford. Bankers are number crunchers and may convince you your sights are too low.

Don't fall for this trick. The numbers may look reasonable on paper, but you're the one who will live financially strapped.

My wife and I had an excellent credit rating when we shopped for a home in 2005. The lender tried to upsell us to a larger mortgage while being pre-approved. We resisted due to unpredictability discussed earlier. Three and a half years later, the economy stalled. If we had taken the self serving advice of the lender, we would be a foreclosure statistic, or at least very "under water." Today, we are neither. We bought what made sense and didn't overtax our finances.

Buying a smaller and lower priced house to upgrade later is also wise. This allows time to build equity while the home increases in value, giving you more money for the next one.

CARS

Earlier we mentioned selling the car to slay the debt monster and be victorious with money. Sell my car? Are you nuts? No. But look at some hard numbers, you may wonder if you lost touch with reality when buying your shiny ride.

Data from Edmunds.com shows depreciation for a new Ford F 150 pickup. This popular model costs $50,154 new in their example. After one year, you lose $14,349 in value. Who cares? Most people keep it longer than one year. Okay, fair enough.

After the fourth year, you will have $23,244 less in value. Depreciation is called the "silent thief" and this burglar is good at what he does.

I won't bore you with endless numbers. When you purchase new, you suffer a 50% - 60% decrease in value in five short years for that very cool truck. You are pouring money into an asset with declining worth. $23000 later, it may not look as cool. If it seems like chump change, my hat is off to you. If you live in the real world like I do, a huge pile of $20 bills makes life easier and more fun.

With depreciation and loan interest factored in, this is a terrible deal. I've paid cash for used cars and kept them for years of great service. Dealers would have you believe without a car payment, you'll be on the side of the road waiting for a tow truck constantly. Not true. Their commissions may take a hit, but you'll be fine. To have success in finances, resist dumping dollars into the black hole of depreciation. Consider buying older and paying cash to sidestep the drain on your money.

LEASES

The only thing worse than financing a new car is leasing one. Leases offer low monthly payments but you'll never own the car. The contracts are complicated and the clauses and requirements are tilted to favor the dealer. There are mileage limitations, and the fees add up considerably should you exceed them.

You are responsible for all maintenance and repairs. The leasing company allows for normal wear and tear. But "normal" to you may be excessive to the dealer. You'll pay for that too. Many have had to write a check to be able to leave the lot with nothing. After years of payments, you build no equity. The car belongs to the dealer. It's a bad deal. If you have car fever, go home and take a cold shower and rethink it with a clear head the next day. There's a better way to spend the payment. Read on.

INVESTMENTS AND RETIREMENT

Long term saving and investing is a paradox. Young people who benefit the most from investments lack the money to invest. The older ones with money lack enough years for it to grow into a great pile of cash. Millennials and Gen Xers get the biggest bang for their buck, but saving for the future isn't even on the radar. Their cash is in high demand for present needs.

This is another opportunity to break from the crowd and conventional wisdom. A great book to read is *"The Latte Factor, Why you Don't Have to be Rich to Live Rich."* The author David Bach shows how to take small amounts you spend, and redirect it to living your dreams and building great wealth over time. The magic bullet is compound interest and time. The great Albert Einstein said, "Compound interest is the eighth wonder of the world. He who understands it, earns it . . . he who doesn't . . . pays it." These are destiny changing principles. In the book, he gives the example of a latte and muffin in the morning, lunch at a restaurant and an afternoon snack as a typical workday habits and how it can bring you potentially millions of dollars if invested well.

What if you do the same with your car payment? $400 per month invested in the right mutual funds is a game changer. You need transportation and lunches. But consider scaling back and choosing a different path than the crowd. The crowd is broke, in debt and headed for a boring retirement, or a working one (which isn't really retirement).

You don't need to drive junk. Pay cash and bank the dollars you would spend on a car payment. Drive it for a year, trade it with your cash and upgrade. Keep this formula going until you're happy with your car. You'll pay no interest, and if the economy slows, no one can repossess your 'paid for' car. It's a poor strategy to buy an asset that loses value so quickly.

It's important to know you can build wealth. Enlist the help of a reputable investment expert if you're unsure how to start. They can explain the time value of money. Less money invested earlier yields more than greater amounts invested later.

Some people like to demonize the rich. I do not. I want to be one of them. Wealthy people build hospitals and orphanages. Abundance allows people to donate to worthy causes to help the less fortunate. Affluent employers hire people who need work. Broke people don't do these things. Staying poor benefits NO ONE. You can become one of the people who touch lives with your success. Don't be afraid to dream. Think big, acquire wealth. Zig Ziglar said 'if you aim at nothing, you will hit it every time.' Setting goals is important. Start with small manageable goals. When achieved, raise the bar higher. If you reached the first target, you're able to reach the next one. Decide today to own your life.

COLLEGE

One of the biggest outlays of cash is for higher education. Often, people assume a headlong plunge into debt is required to have the life they desire. This is a poor assumption.

There are common myths about college that need dispelled. The first and worst is anyone who wants any level of success in life will attend a four year university immediately after high school. What I dislike most is the implication that anyone who doesn't do it this way won't ever *really* achieve success. This is foolishness.

Many eighteen year olds aren't ready for college in their maturity or finances. If uncertain of the career path, they may acquire a degree that won't serve them, or be stuck with a career they hate. Young people benefit from time to be sure where they are headed. Time is your friend when making huge life decisions.

The other side of the education fallacy reveals a "cookie cutter" mentality. It assumes every person is a perfect candidate for college. Not true. The tendencies, giftings and strengths of a complex human being won't all fit nicely into the academia mold. People with a mechanical aptitude love to work with their hands, others who need to be outdoors would hate working in an office someone else may thrive in. Your outlook, temperament and passions are as unique as your thumbprint. Thousands are wasted each semester for education that won't serve anyone. Evaluate well. Don't ignore a hunch because it takes you in the opposite direction of family and friends' expectations.

By the way, you wouldn't want to live in a world where no one was a plumber, electrician or air conditioning expert. They are valuable assets who maintain civilization as we know it.

Higher education isn't always the avenue to success. Microsoft founder Bill Gates and Apple's Steve Jobs never finished college, neither did Dave Thomas of Wendy's fame. Simply put, it's not for everyone. If you don't fit the mold, you may find more success cutting your own path through the briar patch.

STUDENT LOANS

Another popular lie is the only way to finance college is to borrow money. Many believe it and are buried under a mountain of student loan debt.

The need to move back in with parents kills the exhilaration of graduating. Instead of excitement for the future, the graduate tries to figure out how to pay back thousands of dollars while drawing an entry level wage.

Also, today's job market is far less impressed with college degrees than in past decades.

WORK

There are better ways. One is to work through school. Many already do this but could step up their game. It may be difficult to take on more work hours under a heavy study load, but being in debt until you retire is no picnic either.

To pay for tuition in cash, a student might consider adjusting academic goals. If it took six years to get a four year degree, would it be worth considering? Six years may seem like forever, but it goes fast. As mentioned, the long term perspective is helpful. It's not fun to delay plans, but it's wisdom and maturity to make the hard decisions.

There's another aspect to consider about employment. If you can land a job in your area of study, some companies offer tuition reimbursement as a benefit. They will cover the costs of tuition as long as you maintain a certain grade point average. This is an excellent opportunity as you are earning money for school while getting more classes paid for. It's like doubling your money.

FREE MONEY

Another avenue to finance your goals is applying for scholarships. Millions of dollars in scholarship funds go unused each year. This is a huge pool of available resources. But you need to apply and state your case why you deserve their money. It demands time and work but America is full of generous organizations that can help you reach goals debt free.

IVY LEAGUE OR STATE?

Another consideration for the college bound is where to attend. Many see college as an escape from the authority of home. Prestigious schools several states away are most alluring to gain the distance from family. This might sound adventurous, but it's expensive. Out of state tuition rates are significantly higher than in state.

Add to this the expense of travel home on holidays, and costs rise even more. Attending college in the state you reside goes a long way towards affordability. If you are close enough, you could live at home and save money on the housing expense. If this sounds too boring, promise yourself a tour across

Europe when you graduate as a reward for being smart.

Ivy League schools with their famous football teams and household name comes with a steep price tag. While it may carry some bragging rights, its true value is questionable.

In fact, the money you will earn with the degree from the elite school will be comparable to most state schools. The ambition and talent of the student carry more weight than the alma mater they hail from.

It's an ongoing debate, but the point is you can receive a great education for a fraction of the cost of an Ivy League.

- Be patient, apply uncommon sense to large purchases.
- Dream. Set goals, measure and achieve them.
- Question conventional wisdom about college.

Profile #6
THE COST OF PEER PRESSURE

Meet Rusty. He's single with lots of cool friends and drives an old pickup truck. The paint is wearing a little thin, and the style is outdated. But it's like a reliable old friend and he just plain likes it.

All of his co-workers rib him about his ugly truck. "Step up to the new century," they say. "Get a truck with a navigation system, satellite radio, and a back up camera."

Rusty's proud of his individualistic ways. But over time, he begins to wonder if he looks strange by keeping his old truck.

He worries the individualism has bled over into the "weirdo" zone, which he doesn't want.

Out of curiosity, Rusty decides to shop the market and check prices at new and used dealerships.

Rusty learned a few things in a short time. First, anything popular makes sellers inflexible and reluctant to deal. The prohibitive cost of new trucks makes the used models attractive and in demand.

Secondly, a new pickup truck will cost as much as a comfortable starter home. Except the house will increase in value with time, whereas the truck will steadily drop. You can *live* in the house, but not the truck.

While shopping, Rusty found a five year old Chevrolet that seemed like a possibility. Still, he wasn't comfortable getting rid of the old one. It was a desire but not a need.

A salesman introduced himself and asked some questions, Brad seemed nice enough. Rusty showed him the one he liked and Brad left to crunch some numbers.

After time away, he returns with some figures. It was here Rusty felt like he fell down Alice's rabbit hole.

The salesman says that Rusty can drive away for just over four hundred a month. Of course, this depends on Rusty's credit score and the term he chooses. He could lower the payment by going longer on the life of the loan, but a shorter contract would raise the payment.

As Rusty was digesting this information, Brad said for a little more, he could probably upgrade a model year or two. For only another ninety to a hundred a month, he could have a later model with lower miles. He explained this would make sense, the newer one had a higher blue book value, and a better looking truck in his opinion. For only the price of a pizza a week, he'd drive a newer, better ride. Not a bad deal.

Brad made sense, but Rusty was trying to follow the numbers trail and falling behind fast. Brad threw out numbers in a nonchalant way that made Rusty reluctant to ask for an explanation. He didn't want to appear stupid and make the salesman talk slower or louder, and explain in child like terms what anyone else would have understood.

Rusty's stomach knotted. Nerves, he figured and decided to buy the truck. The payment would be around four hundred per month. "Great" Brad said, "it's a good idea to upgrade before the old truck leaves you stranded."

The surprise came as the deal was about to close. The "around $400" payment grew into $465.

Brad scribbled numbers on a pad and showed Rusty:

$1738 Sales tax

$995 Dealer fee

$180 Title Transfer and Plate

$700 Extended Warranty

The $20,999 truck was now $24,613. Rusty's stomach sank lower as the balance rose. The difference was more than he paid for his old truck. He wanted to back out but felt he had come too far and signed on the X.

Leaving the dealership in a daze, Rusty looked at his old truck one last time and drove away.

Rusty's story teaches many lessons. The first is the necessity to refuse pressure from others. His trendy friends wouldn't be paying for the new truck. Rusty would. He should have kept what he liked. While the world admires individualistic people, the average person hurries to conform to what's popular.

Rusty could have banked the payment for a year or two. This would have helped in two ways.

First, it would have given him a trial run on the payment. Could he afford this much? If he struggled to save the amount, then it would be hard to make the real payment.

Wouldn't it be better to find out before he signed a contract? "Car poor" is a reality today. That's a person who can afford the payment and very little else. Nice car, but no life.

Second, if he saved each month, he could pay cash for the next truck, or at least have a large down payment. This would also buy time until he was sure about the purchase.

Another tip from the story is to understand the dynamic of sales. Years pass between car purchases for the average person. Most people don't buy cars very often.

Salesmen are in their daily world, their environment. It's easy to feel small, like you're swimming in the shark tank. This isn't meant to bash salespeople. There are some great folks working in car sales. But others will sense cluelessness and try to sell a car, whether it's a good fit or not.

Consumers who ask questions and need clarification on details aren't stupid, they're savvy. Never be intimidated by numbers tossed out. Request a breakdown of charges in writing to review at your leisure in your own space. If they're unwilling to commit in writing, it's a good indication you're in the wrong place.

"Walk Away Power" is the power you wield as a car buyer. If you feel pressure or the answers aren't satisfactory, wish them a great day and head to the door. No one yet has been tackled in the parking lot.

Also, it's wise not to be eager to buy a particular car. If they sense you can't live without it, you will not get the best deal. There is someone a few miles away selling cars also. Everyone knows it. The power to walk demonstrates it.

Last, I was always told growing up to sleep on any big decision. I hated that. It didn't make any sense. What would change overnight? Foolish old folks wanted to postpone a commitment because they didn't know what to do.

Like so much advice I've sneered at, I've come to see the value of waiting. It seems counter intuitive. But I have postponed a big decision and knew exactly what to do before my feet were on the floor the next day. Time helped to make the best decision.

Salespeople may say if you don't buy it now, it'll be gone ("Someone will be here in fifteen minutes to buy it.") Probably not true. But if so, no problem. That isn't the last car in the world. Better to take time to decide well than to jump on a deal and live with remorse.

Chapter VII
Keeping it Going!

All we have to decide is what to do with the time that is given us.

— JRR Tolkien

By applying these principles, your finances will improve. With many great endeavors, a plateau is reached over time. This is normal, and no cause to fret. Follow your plan, persistence is key. Congratulate yourself often. You are taking charge and making changes. Success is proof your new habits are working to alter your present and future.

When you make improvements, after initial success, your drive may taper off. Remember that momentum is your friend to keep rolling forward. It's like riding a bike with the wind at your back. Here are a few ideas to keep the drive going, since it's so much easier than restarting from a dead stop.

Stated simply, don't settle for the status quo. Reach higher and be exceptional in your occupation. Too many people see "work" as a four letter word. Statistics show many heart attacks occur on Monday mornings, triggered by stress of a new week.

The fact many Americans drudge through the week longing for the weekend is sad indeed. They are only enjoying 2/7ths of their life. Our friends at Hospice are correct when they say every day is a gift. If you achieve financial contentment, but dread twenty days of your month, it is still less than fulfilling, and below your potential.

The point has two applications to finances. The first is, you will enjoy more prosperity if you love what you do. With a passion for your work, stress is reduced and you'll be in a healthier state of mind. That's good but there's more.

When you use the natural gifts God gave you, you'll be good at what you do and it won't feel like work. You'll be rewarded. Your boss or customers will recognize your talent and prosperity will flow to you.

Making friends with hard work will position you

to receive good things, keep poverty and hunger away and model a great example for your kids.

Our media saturated culture worships at the altar of fun, leisure and hanging out. It displays fantasy as reality and deludes people into a belief their lives should look like that too. The truth is that work makes the down time possible. We're designed to be productive and face challenges, not snooze by the pool for hours.

Many in our culture wait for someone to make their lives better, this is foolishness. YOU are the only person able to elevate your life to a higher plane. It is also you that can wreck it beyond recognition. Good choices are critical for success. Choose well. Make yourself more valuable by working with diligence. Folks notice when someone strives to be exceptional.

If your friends think you're a goober for keeping commitments and always going to work. Then it's obvious; you need different friends!

If you only see dead end jobs available, then it's time to make yourself more valuable and attractive to higher paying employers.

What's your dream? Train for it. Opportunities abound in America. Technical schools, colleges and motivational speakers can shed light on your pursuit.

Where to go and how to get there is your decision. Work it out. You have a gift and a passion. Learn it and use it. When I coach people with their finances, I encourage them to consider where they want to be five years from today. Success includes having a career to be proud of.

FRUGALITY

You're building a financial house to be proud of and to serve you well. In a real home, it's important to keep good things inside. For example, you may have a state of the art cooling unit to blast frigid air all summer, but if you have gaps around the windows or leave a door open it won't be comfortable long.

You can fill the kitchen with great food but leave them on the counter to spoil and you worked for nothing. A leaky garden hose is a waste of water.

It's the same with money. Careful spending leaves more to work with.

Working diligently keeps money flowing into your account. Restricting the funds from leaving keeps it in your plan longer.

Frugality helps you to do that. It's an old-fashioned, wealth building trait whose time to reemerge is long overdue. Being frugal doesn't mean you never spend money or have fun. Rather, a firm grasp of money's value and how it improves life helps you think about purchases and resist throwing money down a hole. Let Congress do that. They're better at it anyway.

You need to purchase things. But where to buy, and how much you pay are decisions where frugal stars shine.

Become frugal by anticipating purchases. If you receive signals that the lawn mower is nearing the end of its life, start shopping now. Waiting until you need one *today,* eliminates options and forces you to pay full retail. There's a slim chance of a big sale on the day the old one dies. Time is a friend and keeps pressure away from the decision making process.

Having time to shop saves cash. With more time, there are more options to explore. If you know you'll need a power saw and have time to look for a deal. Instead of going directly to the big box stores and shelling out $120.00 or more, explore alternatives.

BUYING USED

One possibility is the pawn shop. A bargain hunter can find deals but must be willing to offer low and negotiate. Your position is strengthened with "walk away power." Show you're aware of many of these things for sale, and just looking a great deal, you'll negotiate a fair trade. But if body language reveals 'I gotta have it', you'll pay top dollar.

If haggling isn't your forte, yard sales, flea markets, and estate auctions are also bargain opportunities. The Internet offers options as well. Craigslist sells almost everything. It takes time to navigate the ads, but I've bought cars, trucks, juicers, computers and more over the years. I found some *great* deals too. Just remember to use caution and meet in a public place. (Never share account info or wire money for a purchase.) If that doesn't appeal to you, try Ebay or Amazon.com. You can usually find exactly what you're looking for, delivered to your door.

You may ask, "Why would I want someone else's junk? I can buy new and know what I'm getting." You can. But you will pay *full* retail plus tax. Remember, the goal is to restrict outgoing dollars.

In America, consumers buy things they like, but don't need. When the novelty wears off, the "must have" becomes a dust collector in the attic. You find it and pay 20% of its original value. Not a bad deal. I've purchased barely used items for pennies on the dollar. I encourage you to find your inner "cheapskate" and see how much you can save buying "previously owned."

Thrift stores and consignment shops offer savings on clothing and furniture. There are few things that can't be found used. Polish your bartering skills and keep more money in your spending plan. If it's not for you, no worries. Continue to buy retail and find different ways to save.

OPTIONS

Money organization brings several benefits. There is contentment, confidence and a legacy to name a few.

Perhaps the best one is options. Wise management of resources gives you a wider horizon than the average person.

People often make poor decisions because their backs are against the wall. When an urgent need arises and they have no savings, they make bad deals they would normally avoid.

Sound management moves your back *away* from the wall. It puts distance between you and despair. The breathing room is great but it gets better.

Orderly finances offer larger options.

For example, thousands of moms go to work everyday, and leave little ones at a daycare center. Some are fine with the arrangement, but many are not. The ones who aren't content may resent the need to work. They feel like they're trading precious moments for a paycheck. Some fear they miss the seasons and nuances of a child growing up, to work a job they don't like much. It can be a bad trade and make an employee feel more like a slave. A clean and orderly moneyhouse empowers you with options, regardless of which way you choose.

You'll be able to create the life you envision. There will be sacrifices and details to figure out, but it's possible when not under the thumb of loans and car payments. It's exciting to decide the future.

I know it's possible because my wife and I pulled it off years ago when our kids were young. We had two incomes but my wife hated that the kids' hours were spent with a stranger who was a good caregiver, but didn't love them like Mama did. We were able to shave a little here, amputate that, sacrifice some and make it work.

In retrospect, our kids are better off than they would have been. I wouldn't change anything. Our family is close and our kids secure and productive adults. It was worth the lifestyle reduction and driving a "beater" for a few years.

Another option is: anything you're passionate about. Like to travel? If you want to see exotic places and destinations, having your money act together makes it possible. You'll be able to save consistently and pay for those long flights around the globe.

Frugality and budgets aren't about living on a shoestring and never having fun. It's the opposite. Because you make sacrifices, and monitor each dollar, you're able to follow your heart's desire, whatever it leads. Financial responsibility enables you to live an enviable life. You direct the dollar power where you desire, not enriching the credit companies.

There's a time benefit as well. If you can shrink your money outlay, and be comfortable on less income, you'll have *time* options.

Without the need of a second job or overtime, you decide how to spend the surplus hours. You may kayak down a river while co-workers make one more deal at a weekend meeting.

If you're a reader, spend long weekends in a window seat reading the inspiration of your choice. If you're a car nut, restore a '62 Cadillac convertible.

The point? You have options when not a hamster on a wheel, working more than you want to because you need every dime. It provides margin in your schedule. Your time is your life so be careful where it's committed.

We should all work but it's easy to get out of balance and over work because of money stress.

Handling money well has no downside (unless it's broke friends who think you're strange), only benefits and options.

MINIMALISM

In a similar vein as frugality, a movement afoot is gaining momentum. Minimalism is a lifestyle where a person keeps only the important necessities. They sell or give away extra items they don't need. It is intentionally simplifying their lives and homes. It's easier to be organized when there is less to manage.

It is making war on clutter and piles of things we all seem to collect.

The multi billion dollar self storage business is an indication we're due for a simplification trend.

Another aspect of the new mentality is to shrink living areas. Smaller homes with more efficient use of space. Some get on board for environmental reasons. For others, it's time benefits, less to find, clean and store.

The movement isn't occurring in any third world country, this is decidedly a western civilization phenomenon. We're the ones with things we don't remember buying. Your new, cutting edge, 'talk of the town' smartphone or award winning new car is being replaced in a few months. Minimalism is the "Emergency Stop Button" on this crazy train. It's the date when you have the awkward conversation and break it off with the 'keep up with the Jones' mentality.

"It's not you. It's me, simplicity beats insanity, so we're through."

The "less is more" mindset is a great tool for your moneyhouse. Less to buy means more options for the rest of the money. In my garage, I have two or three of every tool and gadget. I'm not a compulsive buyer of things, just disorganized. I'll buy the third one because I can't find the first two. I could have saved money with less junk covering up the few things I actually need.

It's easy to see how a smaller home saves cash. Less space to heat and cool, and lower property taxes as well. It's an interesting concept, but be warned if you try it. You will be going against the crowd like entering a stadium after the band went offstage.

The ideas in this book requires courage and fortitude to swim against the current. That's okay. You have what it takes. Make the tougher choices, and you will win.

GIVE IT AWAY

The last thought I'll share is about generosity. We discussed so many ideas to accumulate money and use it well. Why would anyone just give money away when it's difficult to acquire and keep? A similar question might be 'why should I pay off a debt if it has a low interest rate?'. The answer is the same. Because it's a principle, a basic standard for money management.

You would pay the debt regardless of rate to be free of owing money. Likewise, you begin a habit of giving to keep a healthy perspective of finances. A reminder it's not all about us and our desires. We're all part of a larger world with needs that trump and exceed our own. Generosity breaks the cycle of striving for what we want long enough to step back and help someone else reach their goals too.

Since giving isn't required, it generates a sense of gratitude and goodwill for both people. The giver realizes his good fortune and ability to help, and the receiver sees warmth and kindness from a tough world.

Generosity changes the paradigm of money from a board game where the goal is piling up cash and winning, to having wisdom and skills for your needs and to benefit others as well.

It appears counterintuitive. But people who practice generosity always seem to have enough. When you become a giver, money has a way of circling back to you when you need it most. While I can't explain how it works, I just know it does.

- Learn the lost art of frugality to retain dollars.
- Dream. Be excited about the options money creates.
- Less is more.
- Practice generosity.

Profile #7
WHERE'S ALL THE MONEY?

If you surveyed people who struggle with money, you would find a common denominator in their stories. While details vary, the underlying theme would be a lack of sufficient funds to feel successful with money. It's rare for people to think they spend too much but rather, just earn too little.

In truth, I have been there myself. I remember complaining out loud how I always seem to be "just this much short" of what I need. It's human nature to search for a scapegoat for our issues; inflation, greedy corporations or the government picking our pocket. Or maybe just dumb luck, something goes sideways right when we thought we had a little extra.

'Not enough money' is a poor assumption and I can prove it.

Athletes. In particular, broke athletes. A quick internet search will reveal a long list of smart, talented sports celebrities who went broke or filed for bankruptcy protection. We aren't discussing a "good wage earner," but people earning multiple millions of dollars. In some cases, multiple tens of millions. They believed the lie they would never have to be concerned about money again. Not true. When you buy Ferraris and yachts, the balance of a dizzying amount of money falls pretty quickly. Instead of a lifetime of security and prosperity, these young men have years of regret thinking of what they might have done with a huge fortune now squandered. A similar situation are folks who win the lottery, and are instant millionaires. Many bought the same lie and found themselves broke and in despair.

You may be wondering how this applies to your regular, non-millionaire situation. It does. Every single dollar in your plan — counts. Regardless of how large or meager the budget is, each dollar matters. Once spent, the dollar begins its new life with the next owner and doesn't return. You will earn more, but that one is gone.

Our dysfunctional American culture would have you feel like a beggar if you pay attention to small purchases or resist spending money for nonessentials. Some people will laugh at frugality and saving money. Refuse this ridiculous mindset. To be successful and have enough for all your needs, you must scrutinize how money is spent. A large sum of money is comprised of many small amounts. It may seem obvious but some will sneer at the wisdom for fear of looking cheap.

It would have been unthinkable for the athletes mentioned above to compare prices or negotiate a better deal. Lack of concern for the price tag may be part of the prestige in their world, but it didn't serve them well.

The multi-millionaire and a person with $100 has one thing in common. They both have a finite amount of money. It needs to be monitored closely.

This doesn't mean a person can't have nice things or buy something fun. But it does mean that to build wealth, it's necessary to develop the habit of discriminating between what brings good value for your money and an impulse buy that brings temporary satisfaction or declining value.

Questioning where your money goes, coupled with the fortitude to be different than most, will take you a long way toward reaching your goals.

Acknowledgments

I want to recognize and thank the most awesome people in the world, my wife and kids for their unrelenting support and encouragement. I've ignored them for many hours while I stared at a screen, oblivious to my surroundings.

Also, this would have been impossible without the help of fellow writers at WordWeavers (Tampa Chapter.) Especially Jan. Thanks so much.

Writers Roundtable was invaluable as we met countless Sunday nights at Tom and Beth Goehringers' home. We read, critiqued, laughed and encouraged one another. Thank you Michelle for all the insights and ideas.

Sadly, Beth isn't here to see the finished product, but I thank her anyway. We miss you and your help was priceless.

www.ingramcontent.com/pod-product-compliance
Lightning Source LLC
Chambersburg PA
CBHW071512040426
42444CB00008B/1612